Chemical Coping

SOCIOMEDICAL SCIENCE SERIES
Edited by Carl D. Chambers

Chemical Coping
Carl D. Chambers, James A. Inciardi, Harvey M. Siegal

Chemical Coping:
A Report on Legal Drug Use in the United States

By
Carl D. Chambers,
James A. Inciardi,
and
Harvey A. Siegal,
all of the
University of Miami School of Medicine.

S P Books Division of
SPECTRUM PUBLICATIONS, INC.
New York

Distributed by Halsted Press
A Division of John Wiley & Sons

New York   Toronto   London   Sydney

Copyright © 1975 by Spectrum Publications, Inc.

All rights reserved. No part of this book may be reproduced in any form, by photostat, microform, retrieval system, or any other means, without the prior written permission of the publisher.

Spectrum Publications, Inc.
86-19 Sancho Street, Holliswood, New York 11423

Distributed solely by the Halsted Press Division of John Wiley & Sons, Inc., New York.

Library of Congress Cataloging in Publication Data

Chambers, Carl D
   Chemical coping.

   Bibliography: p.
   Includes index.
   1. Psychopharmacology. I. Inciardi, James A., joint author. II. Siegel, Harvey A., joint author. III.   Title.
RM315.C417   615'.78   74-30196
ISBN 0-470-14326-6

Printed in the United States of America
123456789

CONTENTS

INTRODUCTION

There has been much discussion about the *drug problem* and our living in a *drug taking society*. Unfortunately, most of the discussions have either been focused on those who use the illegal psychoactive drugs, e.g., marijuana, heroin, L.S.D., cocaine, etc., rather than those who are regular users of the legal psycho-active drugs such as sleeping pills, tranquilizers, stimulants, and alcohol. It is the intent of this book to focus upon this latter group.

As epidemiologists seeking to determine the extent of substance use in this country and to characterize those most likely to be involved, we have become con-vinced that *the* major drug problem facing all health professionals and all social and behavioral scientists involves those persons who have come to respond habitually to boredom, loneliness, frustration, and stress, with those drugs legally manufactured and available to everyone.

No one knows the *precise* number of people who habitually use chemicals to manage their lives or "cope" with those situations which living itself brings

1

to all of us. No one knows the personal and social
benefits derived from such chemical management and
coping as compared to the *costs* associated with such
adapting behavior. No doubt both are high. The authors
believe this book, based on extensive surveying within
the general population and focusing on legal nonaddic-
tive drug use and misuse, will provide some of the
dimensions of chemical coping in our society as well
as characterize within our society those who are most
involved, thereby providing a base from which the
implications and costs from such coping behaviors can
begin to be formulated.

The information for this book represents our
accumulated experiences derived from conducting personal
interviews with some 30,000 people. Interviews have
been conducted with residents of Arizona, Arkansas,
Delaware, Florida, Indiana, Iowa, Minnesota, Mississippi,
New Jersey, New York, North Dakota, Pennsylvania,
South Carolina, South Dakota, Utah, Wyoming, and
Washington, D.C. We would like to stress the projections
contained within this book represent the *aggregate* of
our experiences in all of these areas and are not meant
to be construed as reflecting what occurs within each
specific locality.

We would like to point out the most dysfunctional
people were *excluded* from our surveys and our subsequent projections. Our data do *not* include persons who
are residents of institutions, e.g., mental hospitals,
nursing homes, jails or penitentiaries, and they do not
include those persons who do not have a permanent
residence, e.g., skid row alcoholics and migrant
workers.

We would also like to stress our awareness that
although we have projected our data to the national
level, these projections have been made without

representation from the major population concentrations on the far west coast. Epidemiologists focusing on that geographical area have indicated the use and misuse of legal substances may be higher than for other parts of the country. While we have no way of confirming this higher rate of use and have no inclination to attempt to refute such a claim, we do not believe the rates would be so high as to significantly alter the projections we are proposing.

Our strategy will be to present the extent of use and the characteristics of those most involved with three general categories of psychoactive substances... prescription drugs, over-the-counter nonprescription drugs and alcohol. This strategy was adopted because even though everyone has *theoretical* access to all three types of drugs, experience, both ours and others, have demonstrated not everyone avails themselves of this access and for all practical purposes access should be viewed as being differential. By comparing and contrasting acutal use, our goal was to characterize *differential use* within each of the three types of drugs.

As a final note, our strategy of presentation relies quite heavily on the presentation of numbers and statistical data displays. While we recognize such a strategy is burdensome to the reader, we have chosen such a procedure because of our belief that the *dimensions* of the "problem" and the *characterization* of the "problem groups" require as much specificity as it is possible to display. Numbers, even if derived from a projected base, are presented for emphasis and are seen as being most critical if the prioritizing and response efforts we hope to see occurring do actually come about.

PART I

Prescriptive Drugs

I

Barbiturates

The barbiturates were first synthesized and introduced into medicine in Germany in 1903. Since that
time more than 2,000 different barbiturates have been
compounded, yet fewer than a dozen of these account
for the bulk of current use. The more common barbiturates include amobarbital (Amytal), pentobarbital
(Nembutal), phenobarbital (Luminal), secobarbital
(Seconal, Tuinal), and butabarbital (Butisol, Fiorinal).
In 1970, some $31,779,000 were spent on the barbiturates
with prescriptions from general practitioners accounting
for 38% and internists accounting for 19% of this total.

Action and Uses

The barbiturates are central nervous system depressants which produce sedative effects at low dose
levels and hypnotic effects at higher dose levels.
As such, the action of the barbiturates can serve to
quiet the user or put him to sleep. In addition, the
barbiturates can be utilized alone or in conjunction
with other drugs as anesthetics in surgical and related
medical situations, for the treatment of acute con-

vulsions associated with drug dependence withdrawal symptoms or various neurological disorders, as antidotes for the toxic reactions of stimulant overdose, and in the diagnosis and attempted therapy of certain psychiatric disorders.

Physiological and Psychological Effects

Barbiturates induce a general depression of neural and muscular activity. In addition, they have a high addiction liability, and tolerance and physical dependence occur from chronic use. The withdrawal syndrome associated with barbiturate addiction is considered more life-threatening than that of opiate drugs and can include convulsions, delirium, and psychosis. Toxic overdose with barbiturates is characterized by coma, a general shock syndrome, and can result in death. Psychic dependence on barbiturates can occur at any dose level. The general psychological and behavioral effects of these drugs, furthermore, are similar in scope and variability to those of alcohol inebriation.

Interactions with Other Drugs

Cross-tolerance exists between the barbiturates and other sedative drugs. This cross-tolerance, however, does not appear to affect the lethal dose, and large quantities of alcohol and barbiturates act in an additive fashion when taken simultaneously, often producing toxic or fatal reactions. Barbiturates are used in conjunction with amphetamines for the purpose of engendering stimulation without the tension-producing effects often associated with amphetamines.

Our survey data indicate the use of barbiturates is widespread throughout the general population. For purposes of describing the extent of this use, we have projected our survey data for the total population above age 13 with the following results:

> In excess of 24 million people (some
> 16% of everyone over the age of 13)
> have taken one or more of the bar-
> biturates.

> As many as 9 million people have
> probably used these drugs within
> the past six months. We project,
> therefore, about one of every three
> people who have *ever* taken a bar-
> biturate has done so recently.

> Probably as many as 4.5 million
> people use one of these prescription
> sedatives on a regular basis.

If one focuses on the regular users of these drugs,
several characteristics emerge:

> Sex does not appear to be a pre-
> dictor of the use of barbiturates.
> For example, females account for
> about 54% of the total population
> above age 13 and 57% of the regular
> users of barbiturates. We believe
> about 3% of all males and all
> females above the age of 13 are
> regular users of barbiturates.

> Age is somewhat related to the use
> of barbiturates with the older age
> groups accounting for a dispropor-
> tionate amount of this use.

Age Group	Projected Distribution of the General Population	Projected Distribution Of Users of Barbiturates
14 - 17	10%	9%
18 - 24	16%	14%
25 - 34	17%	10%
35 - 49	25%	22%
50 and above	32%	45%

The use of barbiturates does *not* appear to be determined by one's socioeconomic class.

Socio-Economic Class	Projected Distribution of the General Population	Projected Distribution of Users of Barbiturates
Upper/Upper Middle	17%	15%
Middle	70%	70%
Lower	13%	15%

The use of barbiturates does *not* appear to be determined by one's race.

Major Races	Projected Distribution of the General Population	Projected Distribution of Users of Barbiturates
White	89%	91%
Black	10%	7%
All Other	1%	2%

Our survey data indicate the major consumers of barbiturates are housewives, retired persons, and other persons who are either unemployed or not a part of the labor force.

Labor Force Categories	Projected Distribution of the General Population	Distribution of Barbiturate Users
Females	(54%)	(57%)
Students	7%	5%
Employed	21%	14%
Unemployed/N. I. L. F.*	26%	38%
Males	(46%)	(43%)
Students	8%	4%
Employed	36%	18%
Unemployed/N. I. L. F.	2%	21%

*NOTE: N.I.L.F. is the abbreviation for Not In The Labor Force which is that category of persons who are not employed and not looking for a job.

Although we are unable to project our data to the national labor force level, a special analysis of data obtained from the general population within all of New York State provides us with an additional indication of the use of barbiturates by the specific job classifications within

RATE OF USE OF BARBITURATES
PER 10,000 PEOPLE

Labor Force Category	Prevalence Rate (Ever Used)	Rate Of Regular Use
Professionals, Technical Workers, Managers and Owners	2,360	260
Clerical and Other White Collar Workers	2,080	160
Skilled, Semi-skilled Workers	1,350	110
Unskilled Workers	1,340	210
Service and Protective Workers	1,520	370
Sales Workers	3,200	1,230
Farmers	630	--
TOTAL Employed	1,890	280
Not Employed Housewives	2,550	240
Other Not Employed	1,730	310
TOTAL Not Employed	2,110	270
TOTAL	2,000	280

the labor force. It is such an analysis which permits us
to speculate that the *rate* of regular use by job classification of barbiturates is highest among persons employed in the sales field and second highest among those
who are employed in service or protective job categories

Problem Indicators

>Our data suggest no more than 85% of
>the regular users of barbiturates obtain
>*all* of these barbiturates with their
>own legal prescription.

>Our data further suggest that no more
>than 75% of the regular users of
>barbiturates take them exactly as they
>were prescribed.

>Over one-third of all the regular users
>of barbiturates are concurrently using
>one or more of the other prescription
>psychoactive medications...usually a
>nonbarbiturate sedative or one of the
>minor tranquilizers.

>About 50% of all regular users of
>barbiturates are also regular users of
>alcohol and 10% can be considered as
>heavy drinkers.

II

Nonbarbiturate Sedatives

What can be said about the barbiturates is generally also appropriate for the nonbarbiturate sedatives. This would be the case whether the examples were for legitimate medical use or the effects of misuse.

While most of these drugs are indeed physically addicting when misused, available evidence suggests this addiction will occur only at dose levels considerably in excess of those therapeutically prescribed. Once addiction has occurred, the abstinence syndrome can include convulsions, delirium, psychoses, and even death unless the detoxification is medically managed.

The more commonly used nonbarbiturate sedatives include: Doriden, Valmid, Placidyl, Noludar, Quaalude, and Soper.

In 1970, some $22,000,000 were spent on the nonbarbiturate sedatives with prescriptions from general practitioners accounting for 30% and internists accounting for 14% of this total.

Our survey data indicate the use of the nonbarbiturate sedatives is less extensive than the use of the barbiturates. Projections from our surveys suggest the

13

following:

> We believe some 4.5 million people
> (some 3% of everyone over the age
> of 13) have taken a nonbarbiturate
> sedative at some time during their
> lives.
>
> We further believe, over a million
> of these people have used these drugs
> within the past six months or about
> one of every nine people who have ever
> used drugs have done so recently.
>
> Probably as many as a third of a
> million people are regular users of
> these drugs.

If one focuses on the regular users of these drugs, several characteristics emerge from our survey projections.

> Males probably use these drugs
> regularly more often than do
> females.

	Projected Distribution of the General Population	Projected Distribution of Users of Non-Barbiturate Sedatives
Males	46%	54%
Females	54%	46%

> Age does *not* appear to be a
> significant variable in the use
> of these drugs.

Age Group	Projected Distribution of the General Population	Projected Distribution of Users of Non-Barbiturate Sedatives
14 - 17	10%	12%
18 - 24	16%	14%
25 - 34	17%	15%
35 - 49	25%	24%
50 and above	32%	35%

One's socioeconomic class position *does* appear to influence whether one uses these drugs. The upper and upper middle classes are proportionately overrepresented among the regular users of nonbarbiturate sedatives.

Socioeconomic Class	Projected Distribution of the General Population	Projected Distribution of Users of Non-Barbiturate Sedatives
Upper/Upper Middle	17%	25%
Middle	70%	61%
Lower	13%	14%

One's race *does* appear to influence whether one uses these drugs. Blacks are proportionately overrepresented among regular users of nonbarbiturate sedatives.

Major Races	Projected Distribution of the General Population	Projected Distribution of Users of Non-Barbiturate Sedatives
White	89%	81%
Black	10%	18%
All Other	1%	< 1%

The major overrepresentations of regular users of the nonbarbiturate sedatives occur among housewives, retired persons, and other persons who are either unemployed or not a part of the labor force.

Labor Force Categories	Projected Distribution of the General Population	Projected Distribution of Users of Non-Barbiturate Sedatives
Females	(54%)	(46%)
Students	7%	5%
Employed	21%	11%
Unemployed/ N. I. L. F.	26%	30%
Males	(46%)	(54%)
Students	8%	7%
Employed	36%	30%
Unemployed/ N. I. L. F.	2%	17%

A special analysis of data obtained within the general population of New York State provides us with an additional indication of who is involved with these drugs on a regular basis. Focusing on specific classifications of workers, this analysis suggests housewives and unskilled workers are more likely to use these drugs on a regular basis than any of the other worker categories. Clerical and other white collar workers appear to be the least likely to regularly use these drugs.

RATE OF USE OF NON-BARBITURATE SEDATIVES
PER 10,000 PEOPLE

Labor Force Category	Prevalence Rate (Ever Used)	Rate Of Regular Use
Professionals, Technical Workers, Managers and Owners	1,120	120
Clerical and Other White Collar Workers	870	80
Skilled, Semi-skilled Workers	760	90
Unskilled Workers	480	180
Service and Protective Workers	930	110
Sales Workers	670	20
Farmers	320	160
TOTAL Employed	860	100
Not Employed Housewives	860	180
Other Not Employed	850	140
TOTAL Not Employed	850	160
TOTAL	860	130

Problem Indicators

Based on our total survey data, we believe only some 70% of the regular users of the nonbarbiturate sedatives obtain *all* of these drugs with their own legal prescription. In addition, only about 70% of all these regular users take them exactly as they were prescribed.

One can expect over one-third of all the regular users of the nonbarbiturate sedatives to also use another of the prescription psychoactive medications. This concurrent regular use most frequently involves the barbiturates and/or the minor tranquilizers.

Some 70% of the regular users of non-barbiturate sedatives are also regular users of alcohol but less than 10% are heavy drinkers.

III

Minor Tranquilizers

The minor tranquilizers refer to a group anxiolytic sedatives that were introduced into medical practice during the 1950's. They are designated as *minor* tranquilizers, effective in the reduction of anxiety and tension, as opposed to the *major* tranquilizers which are antipsychotic drugs employed in the treatment of severe mental disorders. Librium, Valium, Miltown, and Equanil are the most widely prescribed of the minor tranquilizers.

In 1970, some $357,300,000 were spent on these minor tranquilizers with prescriptions from general practitioners accounting for 32% and prescriptions from internists accounting for 17% of the total.

Action and Uses

The minor tranquilizers have a depressant effect on the central nervous system. They are widely used in current medical practice, typically prescribed for patients suffering from anxiety, tension, behavioral excitement, and insomnia, In addition, these drugs have applications in the treatment of lower back pain,

19

convulsive disorders, and withdrawal symptoms of opiate and alcohol dependence.

Physiological and Psychological Effects

The side effects of these drugs can include drowsiness, ataxia, lethargy, skin rashes, nausea, diminished sex interest, menstrual and ovulatory irregularities, and blood abnormalities. High doses of the minor tranquilizers can depress respiratory functioning, and can produce unconsciousness, coma, and death. Tolerance usually develops to most of the effects of these drugs and doses are typically increased in order to maintain the desired effects. Physical dependence can occur with long-term use at excessive doses, and the abstinence syndrome following the abrupt withdrawal of an addicting dose level can be life-threatening. Psychological effects of the minor tranquilizers are similar to those of alcohol and the sedatives. Therapeutic doses precipitate relaxation, feelings of well-being, and sometimes loss of inhibition; excessive quantities of the drugs can cause disorientation, confusion, memory impairment, trances, double vision, and personality alterations.

Interactions with Other Drugs

Cross-tolerance and cross-dependence exist with minor tranquilizers and other sedating drugs. This cross-tolerance does not affect the lethal dose, and the consumption of these drugs along with alcohol and barbiturates have additive effects which can produce toxic or fatal reactions.

Our survey data indicate the use of the minor tranquilizers to be more extensive than the use of any other group of prescription psychoactive medications. Projections from our surveys suggest the following:

More than 20,000,000 people (some 18% of everyone over the age of 13) have at sometime used one of the prescription minor tranquilizers.

More than 13,500,000 people can be considered as *recent* users of these drugs having used them within the last six months.

Probably as many as 5,000,000 people are regular users of minor tranqilizers.

It is for these 5,000,000 people we have attempted to provide a description. Projecting from our surveys, the following characteristics have been noted:

Females are significantly over-represented among those who regularly seek to reduce anxiety and tension with the minor tranquilizers.

	Projected Distribution of the General Population	Projected Distribution of Users of Minor Tranquilizers
Males	46%	33%
Females	54%	67%

Age is a significant variable in the use of the minor tranquilizers... overrepresentation occurs from age 35 and above but is most prevalent for persons above age 50.

Age Group	Projected Distribution of the General Population	Projected Distribution of Users of Minor Tranquilizers
14 - 17	10%	3%
18 - 24	16%	10%
25 - 34	17%	15%
35 - 49	25%	29%
50 and above	32%	44%

There is a slight relationship
between socioeconomic class position
and the use of minor tranquilizers
with the upper and upper middle classes
being somewhat overrepresented.

Socioeconomic Class	Projected Distribution of the General Population	Projected Distribution of Users of Minor Tranquilizers
Upper/Upper Middle	17%	23%
Middle	70%	65%
Lower	13%	12%

One's race does appear to influence
whether one uses prescription minor
tranquilizers to cope with anxiety
and tension. Blacks are proportionately
underrepresented among those who
regularly use these drugs.

Major Races	Projected Distribution of the General Population	Projected Distribution of Users of Minor Tranquilizers
White	89%	94%
Black	10%	6%
All Other	1%	< 1%

The major overrepresentations of
regular users of the minor tranquilizers occur among housewives,
retired persons, and other persons
who are either unemployed or not
a part of the labor force.

Labor Force Categories	Projected Distribution of the General Population	Projected Distribution of Users of Minor Tranquilizers
Females	(54%)	(67%)
Students	7%	3%
Employed	21%	18%
Unemployed/ N. I. L. F.	26%	46%
Males	(46%)	(33%)
Students	8%	2%
Employed	36%	18%
Unemployed/ N. I. L. F.	2%	13%

Again our special analysis of data obtained from the general population survey of New York State provides us with an additional indication of who is involved with these drugs on a regular basis. Focusing on specific classifications of workers, this analysis suggests housewives and clerical/other white collar workers are more likely to be regular users of minor tranquilizers than any of the other worker categories. Skilled and semi-skilled workers are probably the least likely to use these drugs.

Problem Indicators

> Based on our total survey data we believe over 90% of all regular users of minor tranquilizers obtain *all* of these drugs with their own legal prescription but that only about 70% take them exactly as they were prescribed.
>
> Only about 15% of those who regularly use these drugs concurrently use other prescription psychoactive drugs on a regular basis. If another drug is used concurrently, it is usually one of the sedatives.

Only about 40% of the regular
users of minor tranquilizers are
also regular users of alcohol and
about 15% are heavy drinkers.

RATE OF USE OF MINOR TRANQUILIZERS
PER 10,000 PEOPLE

Labor Force Category	Prevalence Rate (Ever Used)	Rate Of Regular Use
Professionals, Technical Workers, Managers and Owners	2,310	300
Clerical and Other White Collar Workers	2,320	570
Skilled, Semi-skilled Workers	1,550	150
Unskilled Workers	1,410	310
Service and Protective Workers	1,750	430
Sales Workers	2,500	430
Farmers	320	--
TOTAL Employed	1,950	320
Not Employed Housewives	2,630	530
Other Not Employed	1,460	380
TOTAL Not Employed	2,040	460
TOTAL	1,980	380

IV

Major
Tranquilizers

The major tranquilizers, chemically classified in the
phenothiazine group of drugs, were first synthesized
during the 1880's and were later expanded during the
1950's and 1960's for the treatment of psychomotor
excitement and manic states.

The more common of the major tranquilizers are
Thorazine, Compazine, Stelazine, and Mellaril.

Major tranquilizers typically precipitate depressant
effects on the central nervous system, and their potent
sedative actions have significant implications in the
treatment of acute and chronic psychoses. Used for this
purpose, they reduce panic, fear, hostility, agitation,
and adverse reactions to hallucinations and delusions.
Major tranquilizers may also serve to regularize
thinking and ameliorate disorganized behavioral patterns.

Projecting from our survey data, we believe some
4,500,000 people (about 3% of everyone above the age of
13) have at sometime used a major tranquilizer, about
1,500,000 people have done so recently and somewhere
around 900,000 people are current regular users of
these drugs. We have attempted to characterize these

current regular users of the major tranquilizers with the following results.

Females are significantly over-represented among those who regularly use the major tran-quilizers.

	Projected Distribution of the General Population	Projected Distribution of Users of Major Tranquilizers
Males	46%	38%
Females	54%	62%

The regular use of major tran-quilizers appears to be propor-tionately distributed throughout all age groups.

Age Group	Projected Distribution of the General Population	Projected Distribution of Users of Major Tranquilizers
14 - 17	10%	9%
18 - 24	16%	17%
25 - 34	17%	14%
35 - 49	25%	29%
50 and above	32%	31%

Persons in the higher socio-economic groups are somewhat overrepresented among regular users of major tranquilizers.

Socio-economic Class	Projected Distribution of the General Population	Projected Distribution of Users of Major Tranquilizers
Upper/Upper Middle	17%	22%
Middle	70%	64%
Lower	13%	14%

The regular use of major tranquilizers appear to be proportionately distributed throughout the major races although Blacks may be somewhat underrepresented.

Major Races	Projected Distribution of the General Population	Projected Distribution of Users of Major Tranquilizers
White	89%	92%
Black	10%	8%
All Other	1%	< 1%

Not unexpectedly, the major portion of regular consumers of the major tranquilizers were found to be unemployed persons or persons who are not considered to be a part of the labor force, not employed housewives, retired persons, etc.

Labor Force Categories	Projected Distribution of the General Population	Projected Distribution of Users of Major Tranquilizers
Females	(54%)	(62%)
Students	7%	5%
Employed	21%	12%
Unemployed/ N.I.L.F.	26%	45%
Males	(46%)	(38%)
Students	8%	4%
Employed	36%	12%
Unemployed/ N.I.L.F.	2%	22%

Based on our special analysis of the New York State survey concerning the rate of regular use of major tranzuilizers within various worker categories, it becomes possible to rank the regular users of these drugs. Sales workers were found to have the highest rate of persons currently using these drugs on a regular basis followed by those workers in clerical or other white collar jobs. It is interesting to note, however,

RATE OF USE OF MAJOR TRANQUILIZERS
PER 10,000 PEOPLE

Labor Force Category	Prevalence Rate (Ever Used)	Rate of Regular Use
Professionals, Technical Workers, Managers and Owners	430	20
Clerical and Other White Collar Workers	460	140
Skilled, Semi-skilled Workers	260	60
Unskilled Workers	370	30
Service and Protective Workers	220	50
Sales Workers	210	210
Farmers	310	--
TOTAL Employed	320	70
Not Employed Housewives	300	40
Other Not Employed	320	60
TOTAL Not Employed	310	50
TOTAL	320	60

that the prevalency rate for ever having used the major
tranquilizers was the highest for clerical workers and
second highest for professionals/technical wirkers/
managers/business owners.

Problem Indicators

> We believe about 85% of the regular
> users of major tranquilizers obtain
> *all* of their drugs with their own
> legal prescription but that only about
> 80% take these drugs exactly as they
> are prescribed.
>
> Regular users of major tranquilizers
> normally do *not* regularly use any
> other drugs. If they do, it is usually
> in combination with a minor tran-
> quilizer or a sedative.
>
> Only about 25% of the regular users
> of major tranquilizers drink alcohol
> but those who do are normally heavy
> drinkers.

V

Antidepressants

The introduction of antidepressants some 15 years ago has greatly facilitated the management of a wide variety of depressive states. Generally known as mood elevators, these drugs have chemical structures quite different from the amphetamines and have largely replaced them in the treatment of depression.

In clinical practice antidepressants are continued for three to six months after optimal improvement in the patient's condition has been attained. They are then gradually withdrawn. Tolerance and physical dependence to these substances have yet to be documented.

A wide variety of undesirable effects have been reported with the use of antidepressant drugs. The type of reaction tends to depend on the compound used. Adverse reactions most commonly reported include blurred vision, dizziness, hypotension, dry mouth, and increased sweating. Some of these would of course retard the individual's physical performance capability.

The antidepressants potentiate the effects of alcohol, amphetamines, sedatives, and a number of other substances. Care must be exercised when such compounds and the antidepressants are used concurrently.

In 1970, some $57,000,000 were spent on anti-depressants with prescriptions from general practitioners accounting for 16% of the total, internists accounting for 10% of the total and psychiatrists accounting for almost 60% of the total. The most widely prescribed of the antidepressants are Elavil, Tofranil, and Sinequan.

The use of antidepressants is the least prevalent of all the prescribed psychoactive medications. Projections from our surveys suggest the following involvements:

> Only some 3,000,000 people (less than 2% of everyone over the age of 13) have ever used one of these antidepressants.
>
> About 1,000,000 people can be con-sidered as recent users of these drugs having used them within the past six months. This does suggest, however, that one of every three people who have ever used them have done so recently.
>
> Probably 500,000 people are regular users of the antidepressants.

It is for these some 500,000 people we have attempted to provide a description. Projecting from our surveys, the following characteristics have been noted.

> Sex does not appear to be a sig-nificant predictor of the use of antidepressants although females are somewhat overrepresented.

	Projected Distribution of the General Population	Projected Distribution of Users of Antidepressants
Males	46%	42%
Females	54%	58%

The use of antidepressants is related
to age with the major consumers being
above age 50.

Age Group	Projected Distribution of the General Population	Projected Distribution of Users of Antidepressants
14 - 17	10%	3%
18 - 24	16%	11%
25 - 34	17%	16%
35 - 49	25%	21%
50 and above	32%	49%

The use of antidepressants does not
appear to be significantly related
to socioeconomic status.

Socioeconomic Class	Projected Distribution of the General Population	Projected Distribution of Users of Antidepressants
Upper/Upper Middle	17%	14%
Middle	70%	69%
Lower	13%	17%

The use of antidepressants is
related to race with Blacks being
significantly underrepresented
among those who do use these drugs.

Major Races	Projected Distribution of the General Population	Projected Distribution of Users of Antidepressants
White	89%	94%
Black	10%	5%
All Other	1%	< 1%

The major overrepresentations of regular users of antidepressants occur among housewives, retired persons, and other persons who are either unemployed or not part of the labor force.

Labor Force Categories	Projected Distribution of the General Population	Projected Distribution of Users of Antidepressants
Females	(54%)	(58%)
Students	7%	3%
Employed	21%	19%
Unemployed/ N. I. L. F.	26%	36%
Males	(46%)	(42%)
Students	8%	2%
Employed	36%	23%
Unemployed/ N. I. L. F.	2%	17%

The special analysis of data obtained within the general population of New York State provides us with an additional indication of who is involved with these drugs on a regular basis. Focusing on specific classifications of workers, this analysis confirms that housewives are more likely to use these drugs on a regular basis than any other category of worker.

Problem Indicators

We believe most regular users of antidepressants (over 85% obtain *all* of these drugs with their own legal prescription but that as many as 20% do *not* take the drugs as they are prescribed.

One can expect half of those who regularly use antidepressants to concurrently use other prescription psychoactive drugs on a regular basis, usually sedatives or minor tranquilizers.

Only about 20% of the regular users of antidepressants are regular alcohol users and less than 10% can be considered as heavy drinkers.

RATE OF USE OF ANTIDEPRESSANTS
PER 10,000 PEOPLE

Labor Force Category	Prevalence Rate (Ever Used)	Rate Of Regular Use
Professionals, Technical Workers, Managers and Owners	210	--
Clerical and Other White Collar Workers	210	30
Skilled, Semi-skilled Workers	230	30
Unskilled Workers	150	30
Service and Protective Workers	70	--
Sales Workers	170	--
Farmers	--	--
TOTAL Employed	200	20
Not Employed Housewives	380	60
Other Not Employed	250	20
TOTAL Not Employed	310	40
TOTAL	250	30

VI

Amphetamines

We have limited our inquiry into the use of prescription stimulants to amphetamines and amphetamine base stimulants and hunger suppressants.

The amphetamines are potent central nervous system stimulants. They are pharmacologically and chemically similar to a larger group of substances known as *pressor* or *sympathomimetic* amines, which have an action in the body similar to the stimulating effects of adrenaline. Amphetamines were initially synthesized during the latter part of the 19th century, but were not used extensively in medical practice until the 1930's.

In 1970, some $85,000,000 were spent on the amphetamines and amphetamine base stimulants and hunger suppressants. Prescriptions from general practitioners accounted for 62% of this total and internists accounted for an additional 11%.

Action and Uses

Amphetamines have been indicated in the clinical management of psychiatric depression, obesity and weight control, chronic fatigue and narcolepsy, hyperkinetic activity disorders in children, as an analeptic in sedative overdose, and as a local vaso-constrictor for inflamed mucosal membranes. Recently, however, the therapeutic applications of the amphe-tamines have been notably curtailed. Amphetamines are still indicated for the clinical management of narcolepsy and hyperkinesis (both of these are rather rare dis-orders). Their use in wieght control has been seriously questioned since their appetite-suppressing effects endure only a short time and their potential for habituation and psychological dependence is great. Other drugs, furthermore, have been found to be more effective in the management of psychiatric depression and amphetamines are now only rarely used. They will be prescribed only in extraordinary circumstances to diminish fatigue.

Physiological and Psychological Effects

The general physiological effects of the amphe-tamines can include increases in both heart beat and vascular tone, relaxation of the gastrointestinal tract and bladder, and the secretion of thick, sparse saliva. Overdosage can produce a hyperthermic condition, convulsions, unconsciousness, coma, and death. Sustained usage leads to the development of tolerance to both the effects of the drug and the toxic level. Side effects include nervousness, insomnia, and hyperactive behavior. There is, as yet, no agreement as to whether any sort of physical addiction occurs, but there is universal acknowledgment that withdrawal after prolonged and/or heavy usage leads to chronic fatigue, excessive drowsiness, and moderate to severe depression. Psychological dependence on amphetamines has been well documented. Amphetamines produce a state of arousal or wakefulness, an increase in all types of

motor and psychic activity, and depression of the
appetite. Psychologically the effects are experienced
as increased energy and self-confidence, a generalized
feeling of well being, and/or elation or euphoria.
Prolonged use of greater than therapeutic doses will
precipitate the emergence of a toxic psychosis
characterized by bizarre mentation and paranoid delusions. Visual and auditory hallucinations have also
been documented.

Interactions with Other Drugs

The amphetamines are frequently used, both clinically
and illicitly, in conjunction, or in alternation, with
a variety of depressant drugs such as sedatives,
alcohol, or heroin. Amphetamines also reportedly
prolong, intensify, or otherwise alter the effects of
other stimulants, sedatives, analgesics, and hallucinogenic drugs.

The amphetamines are typically misused for their
energizing and euphorigenic properties. Self-medication
has been common in groups such as housewives, students,
truck drivers, and factory workers. Although recent
controls placed on these drugs have curtailed their
availability, we have every reason to believe those
persons who used and misused them in the past will
either continue to seek them out or will seek out
other nonamphetamine stimulants.

Pep Pills

For the purposes of our surveys, pep pills were
defined as those prescription amphetamines which were
taken for their energizing effects. We have encountered
only two drugs with any regularity, Benzedrine and
Dexedrine.

Our survey data indicate the admitted use of
amphetamines specifically for their energizing effect

has involved some 6,000,000 people (almost 4% of everyone above the age of 13). We are projecting some
1,500,000 people as recent users and some 750,000
people as being current regular users.

Projecting from our surveys, the following characteristics of the current regular users have been noted:

Males are significantly over-
represented among those who admit
to the regular use of amphetamines
for their energizing effects.

	Projected Distribution of the General Popultation	Projected Distribution of Users of Pep Pills
Males	46%	63%
Females	54%	37%

The use of amphetamine pep pills is
significantly related to age...over
one-half of all regular users are
under the age of 25.

Age Group	Projected Distribution of the General Population	Projected Distribution of Users of Pep Pills
14 - 17	10%	17%
18 - 24	16%	38%
25 - 34	17%	20%
35 - 49	25%	8%
50 and above	32%	17%

The use of amphetamine pep pills
does appear to be related to one's
socioeconomic position with overrepresentations occurring in both
the middle and lower socioeconomic
groups.

Socio-economic Class	Projected Distribution of the General Population	Projected Distribution of Users of Pep Pills
Upper/Upper Middle	17%	9%
Middle	70%	74%
Lower	13%	17%

The use of amphetamine pep pills does not appear to be related to race.

Major Races	Projected Distribution of the General Population	Projected Distribution of Users of Pep Pills
White	89%	88%
Black	10%	9%
All Other	1%	3%

Students and employed persons were not found to be overrepresented in the regular use of amphetamine pep pills. Our data indicate the only significant overrepresentation occurs among unemployed males and/or males who are not in the labor force.

Labor Force Categories	Projected Distribution of the General Population	Projected Distribution of Users of Pep Pills
Females	(54%)	(37%)
Students	7%	5%
Employed	21%	21%
Unemployed/ N. I. L. F.	26%	11%
Males	(46%)	(63%)
Students	8%	9%
Employed	36%	36%
Unemployed/ N. I. L. F.	2%	18%

Our special analysis of data obtained from the general population survey of New York State provides us with an additional indication of who is involved with these drugs on a regular basis. Focusing on specific classifications of employed workers, this analysis suggests sales workers are more likely to be regular users of the amphetamine pep pills although even these workers are less likely to use these drugs than those who are unemployed.

Problem Indicators

The availability of amphetamine pep pills during the period of our surveys (1973-1974) from other than strictly legal sources was quite high. We found only some 30% of the regular users of these drugs obtained all of their own legal prescription. Even among those who did obtain their drugs with a legal prescription, only a third of them took these drugs as they had been prescribed.

At least one-fourth of those who regularly use amphetamines for their stimulating effect can be expected to also be regularly using minor tranquilizers.*

Our data indicate almost all regular users of amphetamine pep pills are also drinkers with about half of them being heavy drinkers.

*Although the use of illegal drugs is not a topic being considered in this book, we have noted that about one half of the regular users of amphetamine pep pills are also regular users of illegal drugs usually marijuana.

RATE OF USE OF AMPHETAMINE PEP PILLS
PER 10,000 PEOPLE

Labor Force Category	Prevalence Rate (Ever Used)	Rate Of Regular Use
Professionals, Technical Workers, Managers and Owners	830	80
Clerical and Other White Collar Workers	700	80
Skilled, Semi-skilled Workers	580	40
Unskilled Workers	610	30
Service and Protective Workers	920	80
Sales Workers	590	140
Farmers	320	--
TOTAL Employed	690	70
Not Employed Housewives	430	30
Other Not Employed	660	160
TOTAL Not Employed	540	90
TOTAL	630	80

Diet Pills

The diet pills most often consist of an amphetamine
in combination with a central nervous system depressant.
When combined this way, the stimulant acts to reduce
appetite and the depressant serves to counteract any
overstimulation which might otherwise occur.

The use of amphetamine-containing diet pills appears
to be closely related to their ability to create a
sense of well being. As such they may be useful when
applied for short periods of time. However, their
long-term effectiveness in weight control has been
properly questioned.

Our survey data indicate the use of amphetamines
ostensibly for their hunger suppressant effects has
involved some 12,000,000 people (some 8% of everyone
above the age of 13). We are projecting some
3,000,000 people as recent users and more than
1,500,000 as current regular users.

Projecting from our surveys, the following characteristics of the current regular users have been noted:

> Females are significantly over-
> represented among those who
> regularly use amphetamines as an
> "aid to weight reduction."

	Projected Distribution of the General Population	Projected Distribution of Users of Diet Pills
Males	46%	22%
Females	54%	78%

> Overrepresentations among the
> regular users of amphetamines for
> "weight control" occurs between
> the ages of 18 and 34.

Age Group	Projected Distribution of the General Population	Projected Distribution of Users of Diet Pills
14 - 17	10%	7%
18 - 24	16%	27%
25 - 34	17%	22%
35 - 49	25%	25%
50 and above	32%	19%

The regular use of amphetamine "diet pills" does not appear to be significantly related to one's socioeconomic status although members of the lower socioeconomic group do appear to be slightly over-represented.

Socio-economic Class	Projected Distribution of the General Population	Projected Distribution of Users of Diet Pills
Upper/Upper Middle	17%	18%
Middle	70%	65%
Lower	13%	17%

The regular use of amphetamine "diet pills" does not appear to be significantly related to one's race.

Major Races	Projected Distribution of the General Population	Projected Distribution of Users of Diet Pills
White	89%	86%
Black	10%	11%
All Other	1%	3%

Our data indicate the major overrepresentations among consumers of
amphetamine "diet pills" are housewives and other females who are
either unemployed, retired, or
otherwise not in the labor force.

Labor Force Categories	Projected Distribution of the General Population	Projected Distribution of Users of Diet Pills
Females	(54%)	(78%)
Students	7%	7%
Employed	21%	22%
Unemployed/ N. I. L. F.	26%	49%
Males	(46%)	(22%)
Students	8%	2%
Employed	36%	18%
Unemployed/ N. I. L. F.	2%	2%

Based on our special analyses of New York State
concerning the rate of regular use of amphetamine
"diet pills" within various worker categories, it becomes possible to rank the regular users of these drugs.
In such an analysis it is possible to show that sales
workers have the highest rate of persons using these
drugs, followed by housewives, clerical/other white
collar workers, and professionals/technical workers/
managers/business owners. Service and protective
workers have the lowest rate of use.

Problem Indicators

Our data suggest that only
about 70% of all regular users
of amphetamine "diet pills" obtain
all of their drugs with their
own legal prescription and only
about 70% of those who do, take
them exactly as they were prescribed.

RATE OF USE OF AMPHETAMINE DIET PILLS
PER 10,000 PEOPLE

Labor Force Category	Prevalence Rate (Ever Used)	Rate Of Regular Use
Professionals, Technical Workers, Managers and Owners	1,130	200
Clerical and Other White Collar Workers	1,440	250
Skilled, Semi-skilled Workers	800	90
Unskilled Workers	770	60
Service and Protective Workers	740	50
Sales Workers	1,330	360
Farmers	160	--
TOTAL Employed	1,020	160
Not Employed Housewives	1,890	270
Other Not Employed	810	80
TOTAL Not Employed	1,330	170
TOTAL	1,150	160

Persons who regularly use the amphetamine base "diet pills" do not normally use any other prescription psychoactive drug on a regular basis.

About one-half of all regular users of amphetamine "diet pills" can be expected to be heavy users of alcohol.

VII

Prescription Psychoactive Drugs— Summary

Using data obtained from more than 30,000 interviews with a cross section of people above the age of 13, we have attempted to show the extent to which our society has become involved in the chemical management of their lives. This section of our presentation has focuses on the extent to which such chemical coping is occurring with the prescription psychoactive drugs (excluding analgesics).

Our analyses have resulted in the following projections:

	Have Ever Used	Recent Users	Regular Users	Regular Users Who Use Two or More Of These Drugs
Barbiturates	24,000,000	9,000,000	4,500,000	1,500,000
Other Sedatives	4,500,000	1,000,000	300,000	100,000
Minor Tranquilizers	20,000,000	13,500,000	5,000,000	750,000
Major Tranquilizers	4,500,000	1,500,000	900,000	(insignificant)
Antidepressants	3,000,000	1,000,000	500,000	250,000
Amphetamine "Pep Pills"	6,000,000	1,500,000	750,000	190,000
Amphetamine "Diet Pills"	12,000,000	3,000,000	1,500,000	(insignificant)

Our analyses would indicate there are as many as 10,350,000 people (about 7% of everyone above the age of 13) who are regularly using at least one of these prescription psychoactive drugs to stimulate, sedate, and tranquilize themselves. It has also been our experience that you can expect about 65% of these people to also be regular users of alcohol and about 10% of them can be classified as heavy drinkers.

If one were to discuss the regular users of the prescription psychoactive drugs in the most general terms, the surveys have shown white females above the age of 35 who enjoy at least a middle class socio-economic status are the major consumers. In addition, these females are normally found to be housewives or other persons not considered to be a part of the labor force.

REGULAR USE OF PRESCRIPTION PSYCHOACTIVE DRUGS AND ALCOHOL

Regular Drug Users	Percent Who Are Regular Drinkers	Percent Who Are Heavy Drinkers
Barbiturates	50%	10%
Other Sedatives	70%	< 10%
Minor Tranquilizers	40%	15%
Major Tranquilizers	35%	10%
Antidepressants	20%	< 10%
Amphetamine "Pep Pills"	> 90%	50%
Amphetamine "Diet Pills"	50%	30%

SIGNIFICANT OVERREPRESENTATIONS

Regular Users	Sex	Age Group	Race Group	Socio-Economic Status	Employment Status	Highest Rate of Regular Use
Barbiturates	None	50 +	None	None	Unemployed N. I. L. F.	Sales Workers Service/ Protective Workers
Other Sedatives	Males	None	Blacks	Upper Upper Middle	Unemployed N. I. L. F.	Housewives Unskilled Workers
Minor Tranquilizers	Females	35 +	Whites	Upper Upper Middle	Unemployed N. I. L. F.	Clerical Housewives

Major Tranquilizers	Females	35 +	None	Upper Upper Middle	Unemployed N.I.L.F.	Sales Worker Clerical
Antide-pressants	None	50 +	Whites	Lower	Unemployed N.I.L.F.	Housewives Clerical Blue Collar Workers
Amphetamine Pep Pills	Males	- 25	None	Middle Lower	Unemployed N.I.L.F.	Sales Workers
Amphetamine Diet Pills	Females	18-34	None	None	Unemployed N.I.L.F.	Sales Workers Housewives

		Females Above Age 13		
		Students	Employed	Not Employed*
A.	Distribution in the General Population	13%	39%	48%
B.	Distribution of Regular Users of:			
	Barbiturates	8%	25%	67%
	Other Sedatives	10%	23%	67%
	Minor Tranquilizers	4%	27%	69%
	Major Tranquilizers	7%	19%	74%
	Antidepressants	4%	33%	62%
	Amphetamine "Pep Pills"	14%	57%	29%
	Amphetamine "Diet Pills"	7%	29%	64%

*Note: Housewives who are not employed outside the home and who are not seeking employment account for 95% of this category.

A special analysis of data obtained from 7,500 interviews conducted throughout New York State permitted us to establish the rate of regular use of these drugs within specific categories of employed and not employed persons. This analysis revealed rates of regular use for the various drugs to be highest most frequently with housewives, sales workers, and clerical/other white collar workers. This analysis also permitted an additional refinement of the characteristics of persons who regularly use these drugs.

CHARACTERISTICS OF REGULAR USERS OF PRESCRIPTION
PSYCHOACTIVE DRUGS AMONG NOT EMPLOYED HOUSEWIVES

Drug	Percent Regular Users	Age Distribution		Race		High School Graduates	
		-25	25+	White	Nonwhite	Yes	No
Barbiturates	2.4%	3%	97%	93%	7%	80%	20%
Other Sedatives	1.8%	-	100%	96%	4%	69%	31%
Minor Tranquilizers	5.3%	3%	97%	81%	19%	68%	32%
Major Tranquilizers	.4%	-	100%	36%	64%	27%	73%
Antidepressants	.6%	-	100%	65%	35%	53%	47%
Amphetamine Pep Pills	.3%	-	100%	88%	12%	63%	37%
Amphetamine Diet Pills	2.7%	15%	85%	65%	35%	58%	42%

CHARACTERISTICS OF REGULAR USERS OF
PRESCRIPTION PSYCHOACTIVE DRUGS AMONG EMPLOYED SALES WORKERS

Drug	Percent Who Are Regular Users		Age Distribution		Race		Sex		High School Graduates		Any Use of the Drug on The Job
			-25	25+	White	Nonwhite	Males	Females	Yes	No	
Barbiturates	12%	71,000	9.9%	90.1%	88.7%	11.3%	57.7%	42.3%	69.0%	31.0%	11.3%
Other Sedatives	<1%	1,000	--	100.0%	100.0%	--	100.0%	--	100.0%	--	100.0%
Minor Tranquilizers	4%	25,000	8.0%	92.0%	100.0%	--	24.0%	76.0%	48.0%	52.0%	36.0%
Major Tranquilizers	2%	12,000	--	100.0%	100.0%	--	--	100.0%	100.0%	--	--
Antidepressants	--	--	--	--	--	--	--	--	--	--	--
Amphetamine Pep Pills	1%	8,000	12.5%	87.5%	50.0%	50.0%	--	100.0%	100.0%	--	100.0%
Amphetamine Diet Pills	4%	21,000	23.8%	76.2%	100.0%	--	28.6%	71.4%	61.9%	38.1%	28.6%

CHARACTERISTICS OF REGULAR USERS OF PRESCRIPTION PSYCHOACTIVE
DRUGS AMONG CLERICAL AND OTHER WHITE COLLAR WORKERS

Drug	Percent Regular Users	Distribution		Race		Sex		High School Graduates		Any Use of the Drug on The Job
		-25	25+	White	Nonwhite	Males	Females	Yes	No	
Barbiturates	2%	4.3%	95.7%	69.6%	30.4%	43.5%	56.5%	91.3%	8.7%	4.3%
Other Sedatives	1%	25.0%	75.0%	91.7%	8.3%	--	100.0%	100.0%	--	16.7%
Minor Tranquilizers	6%	14.8%	85.2%	87.7%	12.3%	14.8%	85.2%	84.0%	16.0%	3.7%
Major Tranquilizers	1%	--	100.0%	100.0%	--	30.0%	70.0%	60.0%	40.0%	15.0%
Antidepressants	< 1%	--	100.0%	100.0%	--	--	100.0%	50.0%	50.0%	--
Amphetamine Pep Pills	1%	25.0%	75.0%	100.0%	--	50.0%	50.0%	100.0%	--	--
Amphetamine Diet Pills	3%	40.0%	60.0%	82.9%	17.1%	2.9%	97.1%	88.6%	11.4%	3.5%

The surveys have clearly established extensive utilization of the barbiturate sedatives and the minor tranquilizers. As many as 24,000,000 people have at some time relied on one of these sedatives and 20,000,000 have sought to tranquilize themselves against the effects of anxiety, stress, or tension. The surveys have indicated probably as many as 4,500,000 people regularly use these sedatives and 5,000,000 people regularly use the minor tranquilizers.

PART II

Over-the-Counter Psychoactive Drugs

VIII

History
of
Self
Medication

Introduction

Over-the-counter or *proprietory* drugs, that is, remedies protected by secrecy or patent and privately managed without public control or supervision, have been known for many centuries in this country. As pharmaceutical preparations traditionally designed for the self-medication of "common" ailments, they have been made available through numerous and broad channels of distribution and have always enjoyed acceptance by the general public. Yet a backward glance through time suggests that their very *proprietory* nature has continually placed a number of them in a medically problematic and hazardous position.

It is intended here to offer a brief history of the development of the major groups of over-the-counter drugs combined with some discussion of their pharmacological actions and medical uses. In addition, material is presented regarding the contemporary use of these drugs within the general population of the United States.

Home Remedies and Medicine Shows

Among the oldest of the proprietory, or patent, medicines was Dover's Powder, a preparation containing 10% opium combined with powdered ipecac (the dried roots of a species of tropical creeping plant). The drug was first prepared in 1709 by Thomas Dover, the physician who had rescued privateer and castaway Alexander Selkirk from the desolate island of Juan Fernandez off the coast of Chile, thus inspiring Daniel Defoe's "Robinson Crusoe." Dr. Dover's powder was among the first and most popular of the countless patent medicines containing opium or morphine that were readily available throughout nineteenth century America. They were sold by the billions in pharmacies, grocery and general stores, from traveling medicine shows, and through the mail, and were marketed under such labels as Ayer's Cherry Pectoral, Mrs. Winslow's Soothing Syrup, McMunn's Elixir, and Godfrey's Cordial. Many of these patent remedies were seductively advertised in all forms of media as "pain killers." "cough mixtures," "soothing syrups," "women's friends," and "consumption cures," while others were recommended for diarrhea, dysentery, colds, cancer, teething, cholera, rheumatism, and pelvic ailments. Furthermore, the drugs were produced from imported opium, as well as from the white opium poppies that were being legally grown in the New England states, in Florida and Louisiana, in the West and Southwest, and in the Confederate States during the Civil War.

The therapeutic nature of the opiates were not only favorably addressed in the popular media, but by the medical profession as well during these early periods of American history. Dr. William Buchan's "Domestic Medicine." for example, published in Philadelphia in

1784 as a practical handbook on simple medicines for
home use, suggested for the treatment of coughs:

> "A cup of an infusion of wild
> poppy leaves and marsh-mellow roots,
> or the flowers of coltsfoot, may
> be taken frequently; or a tea-
> spoonful of the paragoric elixir
> [flowers of benzoine plus opium]
> may be put into the patient's drink
> twice a-day. Spanish infusion
> [liquor combined with the syrup of
> poppy leaves] is also a very proper
> medicine in this case, and may be
> taken in the quantity of a tea-
> cupful three or four times a-day."[1]

Dr. Buchan's treatise on home remedies, which was
republished in several editions, also recommended
tincture of opium or liquid laudanum for the treatment of numerous common ailments, the preparation of
which he outlined as follows:

> "Take of crude opium, two ounces;
> spirituous aromatic water, and
> mountain wine, of each ten ounces.
> Dissolve the opium, sliced, in the
> wine, with a gentle heat, frequently
> stirring it; afterwards add the
> spirit, and strain off the tincture."[2]

The ready availability of the opium-containing
nostrums combined with misleading advertising and a
general consumer ignorance of the drugs' hazards led
to virtually thousands of cases of chronic opium intoxication and dependence during the two decades before and
after the turn of the twentieth century. In 1900, for

---

[1]William Buchan, M.D., "Domestic Medicine: or, a
Treatise on the Prevention and Cure of Diseases by
Regimen and Simple Medicines" (Philadelphia: Crukshank,
Bell and Muir, 1784), pp. 225-6.

[2]Ibid., p. 520.

example, it was estimated that 3,300,000 doses of opium
were sold every month in the State of Vermont alone --
enough to provide every man, woman, and child in that
state with a continuous daily supply of one and one-half
doses. Reports from this period also suggested that the
national population of those who had become physically
dependent on opium well exceeded 200,000.

Other proprietory medications, while not necessarily
hazardous to the consumer, were attractively placed
before an unsuspecting and gullible American public at
the hands of several enterprising and imaginative
hucksters. During the Civil War, for example, salt was
typically produced from brine drawn from wells, and
occasionally the utility of such wells was ruined when a
black oily substance (petroleum) found its way into the
underground reservoirs. One Kentucky businessman
secured a number of these "ruined" salt wells, formed
the American Medical Oil Company, and sold hundreds of
thousands of bottles of the greasy brine as American
Oil, advertising it as an effective remedy for almost
any ailment. Even more dramatic were the efforts of
Samuel M. Kier, the profiteering son of a western
Pennsylvania salt manufacturer. In 1846, when oil began
to flow in quantity from his underground salt deposits,
he initiated an active advertising campaign giving
testimony to the wonderful virtues of Petroleum, or
Rock Oil. A Natural Remedy. Procured From a Well in
Allegheny County, Pa. Four Hundred Feet Below the
Earth's Surface. Kier's salesman, equipped with
ornamented wagons and ready supplies of the wonder oil,
brought the "medicine show" to rural America. By 1858,
Kier's operation had sold some quarter million half-pints
of rock oil remedy at $1 per bottle.

Cocaine, like opium and medical oil, also surfaced
among the patent medicines. After its isolation from

the coca leaf in 1860, cocaine was rapidly noted as a
valuable local anesthetic. Sigmund Freud was known to
have been fascinated by the properties of the drug, and
advocated its use for the treatment of psychological
and nervous tensions. By the latter part of the 1800's
the availability of cocaine in proprietory medications
exposed the public to the ill effects of chronic intoxication, typically involving intense fear and anxiety
often combined with hallucinations and paranoid delusions.

The influences of this phase of the patent medicine
industry endured through the turn of the twentieth
century, reaching its peak just prior to the passage
of the Pure Food and Drug Act in 1906. With the new
legislation, adulterated and misbranded preparations
were prohibited from interstate commerce, and drugs
were placed into two classes -- proprietory and ethical,
or, over-the-counter without prescription and dispen-
sation by prescription only. Subsequent drug control
statutes served to further reduce the availability of
many of the harmful and habit-forming drugs, yet the
problematic nature of numerous over-the-counter medications continues to endure. Controls at the retail
level are typically less complete and comprehensive
than those imposed on wholesalers; federal powers
generally focus only on those drugs moving in interstate
commerce; and finally, the available appropriations
for the enforcement of the food and drug laws are, for
the most part, inadequate when contrasted with the
inordinate number of marginal practices characteristic
in the manufacture, distribution, classification, and
marketing of new pharmaceutical preparations.

Brews Both Familiar and Strange

Common to present day self-medication practices are
a group of preparations known as "parasympathetic

nervous system depressants," or sleep inducers. These
drugs typically incorporate one or more of the "belladonna alkaloids," a group of organic compounds --
Atropa belladonna, *Hyoscyamus niger*, and *Datura
stramonium* -- which freely occur in nature and have
been known for centuries for their strange and stupe-
fying properties.

Atropa belladonna, more commonly known as the deadly
nightshade and organically related to the potato and
eggplant, is a widely distributed plant with star-
shaped flowers, showy red berries, and poisonous
qualities. Its name descends initially from Greek
mythology, from Atropos, the eldest of the Three Fates
who arbitrarily controlled the birth, life, and death
of every man. The designations of Atropos was given by
Linnaeus, the eighteenth century Swedish naturalist who
first described the plant. Belladonna, meaning beauti-
ful woman in Italian, derives from the ancient use of
the drug as an eye beautifier, from its ability to
cause dialation of the pupils when smeared on the eyes
in small doses.

Datura stramonium, more typically referred to as the
jimson weed, Jamestown weed, thornapple, or stink
weed, is a spindly plant generally native to temperate
and tropical regions in both hemispheres. Its common
English name, the jimson weed, derives from the late
eighteenth century from a group of soldiers at Jamestown, Virginia, who cooked and ate the leaves of the
plant and experienced its intoxicating effects.
"Jimson" is seemingly a corruption of "Jamestown."
And it was this plant, according to Plutarch, which
produced fatal effects on the Roman soldiers during
their retreat from the Parthians under Mark Antony in
37 and 38 B.C.

Hyoscyamus niger, or black henbane, has been similarly known for centuries, and was used in ancient
Greece as a poison, to produce madness, and to evoke
prophecies.

These organic biologicals have long since been used
in preparations, portions, and brews both familiar and
strange, many of which fell somewhat beyond the range
of orthodox pharmacology. During the Middle Ages, they
were reputedly used criminally for inducing madness
and for seducing women. Eliphas Levi's "Dogma and
Ritual of Magic," suggests that extracts of henbane
and deadly nightshade were the active ingredients in
many a sorcerer's brew, or were joined in the classic
witch's cauldron with more peculiar substances as toad
skin, moss from the skull of a parricide (one who
murders a relative), or horns from a goat that has
cohabited with a young girl. And these plants were
undoubtedly used in the ancient world in connection
with orgiastic rites characterized by sexual excesses.
One might be reasonably certain that at Bacchanalia,
sexual frenzy was not necessarily produced by plain
fermented grape juice. Intoxication of this order was
more likely the result of doctoring the wine with
leaves or berries of henbane or belladonna.

This type of intoxication, a variety of belladonna
psychosis, is generally produced by two substances
found in these plants -- atropine and scopolamine.
More specifically, atropine can effect severe rises in
blood pressure and stimulation of the cerebral cortex.
Its prolonged use can cause one to become talkative,
to experience disorientation and sometimes hallucinations, followed by depression, stupor, coma, and paral-
ysis of the respiratory system. Scopolamine, more
potent than atropine, can produce euphoria, fatigue,
restlessness, delirium, and hallucinations.

There are extensive accounts of belladonna psychosis
produced by atropine and scopolamine. Standard medical
and psychiatric textbooks carry numerous descriptions
to them, and patients continue to be admitted to hospital
emergency rooms suffering from this drug-induced state.
One of the more unique cases involved the self-poisoning
of a family with hallucinogenic tomatoes during the last
decade. Tomato plants had been grafted to the himson
weed where they grew quite well, but delirium and hallucinations of varying intensity occurred subsequent
to the ingestion of these plants. More acute reactions
have resulted from the use of eye drops containing
atropine. Numerous cases have been reported involving
confusion, visual hallucinations, violent and aggressive
behavior, coma, and convulsions.

Significant hazards to the general public emerge with
respect to those over-the-counter nonprescription medications containing the belladonna alkaloids. Most widespread in this respect are the sleep inducers, and the
more popular products for this purpose which contain
belladonna include Sominex, Sleepeze, Sleep, and Quiet
World. Other over-the-counter preparations containing
the belladonna alkaloids include, to name but a few,
Compoz for nervous tension, Contac for nasal congestion,
and Donnagel for diarrhea.

As for the effectiveness of the sleep inducers, the
question is problematic. For severe insomnia, it is
unlikely that these drugs will be consistently effective
for anyone. And some persons may not find them effective
at all, whatever the type of insomnia they suffer from.
In this behalf, Dr. Louis Lasagna, Professor of Pharmacology and Toxicology at the University of Rochester,
School of Medicine and Dentistry, has written:

"Presumably these drugs have come
to be promoted as hypnotics because
of the drowsiness observed as a side-
effect attendant on their use in the
treatment of allergic disorders and
in the prevention of motion sickness.
How effective are the preparations?
No one really knows."[3]

Caffeine - A Domesticated Drug

Caffeine, a mild stimulant present in coffee, tea,
kola nuts, and cocoa, was introduced to the Western
world during the century after the European discovery
of America. During the two centuries following Columbus's
first voyage, explorers and traders brought coffee from
Arabia and Turkey, tea from China, kola nuts from West
Africa, and cocoa from the West Indies, Mexico, and the
tropical Americas. Of these substances, coffee is the
most widely used; in the United States alone, it has
been so incorporated into our way of life that the
annual consumption of this watery extract of the coffee
bean is equivalent to almost 200 billion doses of caffeine.

Although the story of coffee's introduction and
growth has never been fully documented, myth and fantasy
have offered much information which history failed to
provide. Among the Arabs and Persians, it is related
that a brew of coffee beans was presented to the Pro-
phet Mahomet by the Archangel Gabriel, while others
declare that it was discovered along the west coast of
the Red Sea. Whatever its true origin may be, history
does relate that soon after it had become popular in

[3]Editors of Consumer Reports. "The Medicine Show"
(Mount Vernon, N.Y.: Consumers Union, 1971), p. 67.

the East it was quickly declared as a brew of the devil
and, hence, prohibited. In sixteenth century Egypt, for
example, it was considered contrary to the spirit of
the Koran, and whenever stocks of coffee were found
they were immediately burned. Yet the proscription
against coffee failed to endure and the laws against it
were repealed. By 1551, it was enjoyed by the populations of Asia Minor, Syria, and Persia. Less than a
century later, coffeehouses began to appear throughout
Europe, and in America the first coffeehouse -- opened
in 1689 as the London Coffee House -- appears to have
been established in Boston.

The extreme popularity of coffee stems from the
stimulating effects of its active ingredient -- caffeine.
Caffeine stimulates all portions of the cerebral cortex.
Its main action produces a more rapid and clearer flow
of thought; motor activity is increased and drowsiness
and fatigue are appreciably diminished. These effects
can become evident after the administration of 150 to
250 milligrams of caffeine, the amount contained in one
or two cups of coffee.

Yet caffeine has its hazards. Even in moderate doses,
it can effect the heart rate, heart rhythm, blood vessel
diameter, coronary circulation, blood pressure, and
other bodily functions. Overindulgence in the drug can
result in restlessness and disturbed sleep, cardiac
irregularities, and gastrointestinal irritation. When
taken in extremely large doses, caffeine can be a potent
poison. A fatal dose causes convulsions, followed by
death resulting from respiratory failure. The fatal
caffeine dose in man is estimated at 10 grams -- 70 to
100 cups of coffee.

These severe effects may seem irrelevant to the
average coffee drinker, who rarely drinks more than
several cups at a single sitting. Yet the use of

caffeine in concentrated table form has become a popular American custom. No Doz, for example, an over-the-counter variety of concentrated caffeine contains 100 milligrams of the drug in each tablet. As few as ten tablets simultaneously consumed can initiate the toxic reactions described earlier. Even more potent are Vivarin, containing 200 milligrams per tablet, and Kirkaffeine, containing 250 milligrams per tablet. Other preparations containing concentrated caffeine which can be obtained inexpensively and without prescription include Comeback, Enerjets, Tirend, and Chaser for Hangover.

IX

The
Scope
of
Self
Medication

The Scope of Over-the-Counter Drug Use

Since the introduction of Dover's Powder almost three centuries ago, self-medication with over-the-counter proprietary drugs has remained popular among the American public. Yet only minimal data have been available as to the nature and extent of such drug use. Furthermore, the patchwork of reports which have addressed these phenomena have been limited to gross estimations of total over-the-counter drug consumption, failing to isolate those populations who are the more frequent users of specific medications. In this behalf, commentary is offered here descriptive of contemporary nonprescription drug-taking. Our surveys have focused on the use of those proprietary chemical preparations which are most commonly utilized for coping purposes -- ·for the self-treatment of fatigue, stress, anxiety, depression, and insomnia. Three varieties of drugs are presented: sleep inducers, stimulants, and tranquilizers.

Sleep Inducers

Our survey data indicate that the use of over-the-counter sleep inducers is widespread throughout the

general population of the nation. For purposes of
describing the extent of this use, we have projected
our survey data for the total population above age 13
with the following results:

> In excess of 18 million persons
> (some 12% of everyone over the age
> of 13) have taken one of the pro-
> prietory sleeping medications,
> e.g., Sominex, Sleepeze, Nytol,
> etc.

> As many as 4 million persons have
> probably used these drugs within
> the past six months. Stated some-
> what differently, one of every five
> persons who has ever taken an over-
> the-counter sleeping aid has done
> so during the past six months.

> Probably as many as a million
> people use one of these nonpre-
> scription sleeping medications
> every week.

If one focuses on the recent users, those persons who
have used one of these drugs within the past six months,
several things become obvious.

> Females more frequently than
> males use the nonprescription
> sleeping aids. While females
> account for about 54% of the total
> population, as many as 62% of the
> recent users of these drugs are
> females. Of the some 78 million
> females who are over age 13, we
> believe at least 3% are recent
> users of the over-the-counter
> sleeping aids.

> Age is related to the use of the
> over-the-counter sleeping aids.
> The greater one's age, the greater
> the likelihood one will use these
> drugs.

Age Group	Projected Distribution of the General Population	Projected Distribution of Users of O. T. C. Sleep Inducers
14-17	10%	10%
18-24	16%	13%
25-34	17%	13%
35-49	25%	18%
50 and above	32%	46%

This distribution, as illustrated in Fig. 1, points to some interesting factors in the relationship between age and the use of these drugs. For example, as indicated by the dotted line in the figure, the proportion of users in each group increases as the age of the group increases. Some 10% of the users are under

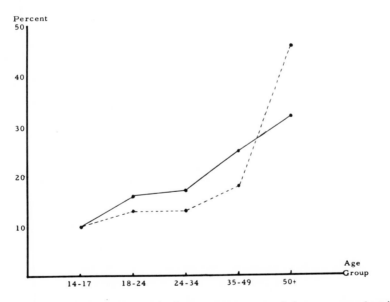

Fig. 1. Current sleep inducer users and base population composition, by age.

age 18 and this slowly increases to 18% for those who
are ages 35 to 49. A startling upsurge appears with
respect to the oldest group, accounting for almost
half (46%) of all recent users of nonprescription sleep
inducers. The solid line in the figure represents the
proportion of persons in the U.S. population who fall
into each of these five age categories. It can be
readily noticed that for all groups under age 50, the
proportions of users in each group and the proportion
of the total population in each group correspond fairly
closely. However, this is clearly not the case with
persons who are ages 50 and above -- they account for
only 32% of the U.S. population yet as much as 46%
of the recent users of nonprescription sleep inducers.
As such, there is a serious overconcentration of sleep
inducer users among persons over age 49 -- some 4%
of all persons in the nation who are age 50 and above
are believed to be recent users of these sleeping medications. The potential health hazards associated with
inappropriate self-medication with these "safe" drugs
by older persons is obvious. As previously noted, many
of these nonprescription sleep inducers contain the
belladonna alkaloids -- central nervous system depressant
agents which can effect significant rises in blood
pressure combined with direct stimulation of the cerebral cortex. Such action on the brain, heart, and
nervous system can be more problematic for this oldest
age group than for any other.

> The use of the nonprescription
> sleeping aids does not appear to
> be determined by one socioeconomic
> class.

Socioeconomic Class	Projected Distribution of the General Population	Projected Distribution of Users of O. T. C. Sleep Inducers
Upper/Upper Middle	17%	15%
Middle	70%	72%
Lower	13%	13%

The use of nonprescription sleeping medications does *not* appear to be determined by one's race.

Major Races	Projected Distribution of the General Population	Projected Distribution of Users of O. T. C. Sleep Inducers
White	89%	88%
Black	10%	11%
All Other	1%	1%

Our survey data indicate the major consumers of these nonprescription sleeping medications are housewives, retired persons, and other persons who are either unemployed or not part of the labor force.

Labor Force Categories	Approximate Distribution of the Population	Distribution of Users of O. T. C. Sleep Inducers
Females	(54%)	(62%)
Students	7%	6%
Employed	21%	14%
Unemployed/N. I. L. F.	26%	42%
Males	(46%)	(38%)
Students	8%	4%
Employed	36%	19%
Unemployed/N. I. L. F.	2%	15%

In summary, the consumption of over-the-counter sleep inducers is indeed widespread throughout our population. One out of every eight persons over age 13 has taken them at one time or another with probably a million people using them every week. The major consumers of these drugs appear to be housewives regardless of their age and persons above the age of 50. The use of these non-prescription sleeping medications appear to be proportionately distributed throughout the socioeconomic groups and in all racial groups.

Stimulants

Our survey data indicate the use of over-the-counter stimulants is somewhat less than the use of sleep inducers. Projecting our findings to the total population of persons above the age of 13, the following involvements are noted:

> Almost 16 million persons (some 11% of everyone over the age of 13) have at some time taken one of the over-the-counter stimulants, e.g., Vivarin, No Doz, etc.

> As many as 3 million persons have probably used these drugs within the past six months. We project, therefore, about one of every five persons who has ever taken one of these stimulants has done so during the past six months.

> Probably as many as a half million people use one of these nonprescription stimulants every week.

The consumers of the over-the-counter stimulants are significantly different than those found to consume nonprescription sleeping aids. Focusing on the recent users of nonprescription stimulants, the following consumer characteristics were noted.

Males more frequently than females
use the nonprescription stimulants.
In fact male involvement with this
class of proprietary drug is almost
twice as great as female involvement.
While males account for about 46% of
the total population above the age of
13, some 65% of the consumers of the
proprietary stimulants are males.
Furthermore, somewhere between 2 and
3% of all males over the age of 13
have recently used one of the over-
the-counter stimulants.

As contrasted with the use of proprietary sedatives, the use of
stimulants is inversely related to
age. The majority of over-the-counter
stimulants are under the age of 25.

Age Group	Projected Distribution of the General Population	Projected Distribution of Users of O. T. C. Stimulants
14-17	10%	16%
18-24	16%	41%
25-34	17%	20%
35-49	25%	15%
50 and above	32%	8%

These data are graphically
described in Fig. 2, illustrating
that recent users of stimulants
are disproportionately distributed
throughout the population. The
dotted line in the figure refers
to the proportion of users in each
age group. While some 16% of them
are under age 18, this dramatically
increases to 41% for 18- to 24-year
olds followed by sharply declining
rates for the older age groups.
The solid line in Fig. 2 represents
the proportion of the U.S. population in each age group. This
comparative progression points to
the disproportionate number of

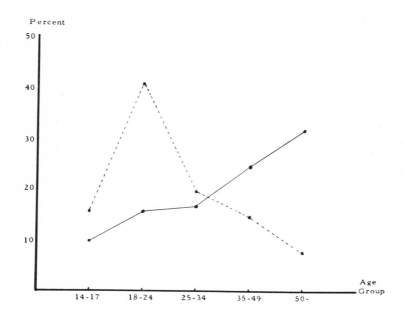

Fig. 2.   Current stimulant users and base population composition, by age.

18- to 24-year olds who use these drugs. While only 16 out of every 100 persons in the base population (over age 13) are 18 to 24 year olds, 41 out of every 100 or almost 1 out of every 2 recent users of these stimulants are ages 18 to 24. Furthermore, more than 4 percent of all 18 to 24 year olds are recent consumers of these drugs.

As noted earlier, the use of nonprescription stimulants -- caffeine in concentrated tablet form -- has become a popular American custom. Students of both sexes have typically used these drugs for lengthening their days and nights when studying or preparing for exams. This has also been the case with many employed males who attempt to chemically reduce fatigue when working long hours, e.g., truck drivers and salesmen.

Our survey data highlight the extent to which such practices are occurring.

> Our survey data indicate the major consumers of these nonprescription stimulants are students of both sexes and employed males. Students account for 23% of all recent users of these drugs and employed males account for an additional 45%.

Labor Force Categories	Approximate Distribution of the Population	Distribution of Users of O. T. C. Stimulants
Males	(46%)	(65%)
Students	8%	13%
Employed	36%	45%
Unemployed/ N. I. L. F.	2%	7%
Females	(54%)	(35%)
Students	7%	10%
Employed	21%	13%
Unemployed/ N. I. L. F.	26%	12%

> With regard to which occupational areas are most effected, the primary overrepresentations among the consumers are in the "blue collar" areas including unskilled, semi-skilled, and skilled workers and among service and sales personnel.

Worker Classification	Approximate Distribution of Total Labor Force	Percent of Total Users of O. T. C. Stimulants
Unskilled	5%	12%
Skilled/Semi- Skilled	29%	34%
White Collar/ Other Clerical	17%	4%
Professionals, Manager, Owners	23%	10%
Service/Sales/Others	26%	40%

The use of nonprescription
stimulants does *not* appear to
be related to one's socioeconomic class.

Socioeconomic Class	Projected Distribution of the General Population	Projected Distribution of Users of O. T. C. Stimulants
Upper/Upper Middle	17%	18%
Middle	70%	70%
Lower	13%	12%

The use of nonprescription
stimulants does *not* appear to
be related to one's race.

Major Race	Projected Distribution of the General Population	Projected Distribution of Users of O. T. C. Stimulants
White	89%	90%
Black	10%	8%
Other	1%	2%

In summary, the consumption of over-the-counter
stimulants is indeed widespread with some 3 million
people having recently used them. Males more than
females and younger persons more than older ones are
most likely to be consumers of these drugs. The use
of nonprescription stimulants appear to be proportionately distributed throughout all of the socioeconomic and race groups. Of significant concern to us
is the finding that almost 60% of the consumers of
these drugs are workers who operate or are around
machinery and who operate motor vehicles. These workers
are at a high risk of becoming exposed to the hazardous
effects, both direct and indirect, of these drugs when
repeatedly ingested. While the caffeine in these
stimulants can relieve drowsiness and offer clearer

thought, such effects are of limited span and dosages must be repeated and increased to maintain the desired state of consciousness. Yet the ingestion of concentrated caffeine in large quantities can initiate cardiac irregularities or even toxic reactions. Not insignificantly, the extended use of these stimulants only masks the fatigued state of the body and cannot fully restore the sensory perception and reflex action that is characteristic of a rested organism.

Tranquilizers

Projections from our surveys indicate a significant proportion of the population has been involved in the consumption of over-the-counter tranquilizers.

> About 15 million persons (some 10% of everyone over the age of 13) have taken one of the proprietary tranquilizing medications, e.g., Compoz, Cope, etc.

> Probably as many as two and a half million people can be considered as *recent* users, having used these drugs within the past six months. Therefore, 1 out of every 4 persons who have *ever* used them have done so recently.

> About a half million individuals use these tranquilizing medications every week.

Focusing on the 2.5 million recent users, the following characterizations were noted.

> Females more frequently than males use the nonprescription tranquilizer drugs for the self treatment of stress, tension, or in the pursuit of other mood alterations. While females account for about 54% of the population above age 13, they account for almost 70% of the consumers of these drugs.

Unlike the consumption of sleeping aids which increases with age (involves more persons in the older age groups), the consumption of the tranquilizing medications decreases with age (involves proportionally fewer persons in the older age groups).

Age Group	Projected Distribution of the General Population	Projected Distribution of Users of O. T. C. Tranquilizers
14-17	10%	15%
18-24	16%	22%
25-34	17%	22%
35-49	25%	19%
50 and above	32%	22%

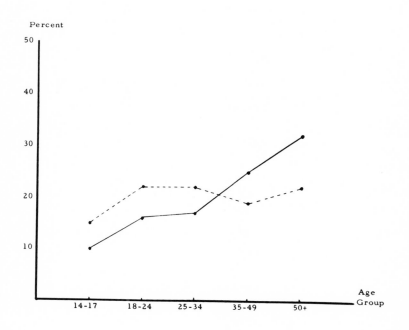

Fig. 3. Current tranquilizer users and base population composition, by age.

The use of the nonprescription tranquilizers *does* appear to be associated with one's socioeconomic class. The higher one's socio-economic status the greater the likelihood one will use these coping medications.

Socio-Economic Class	Projected Distribution of the General Population	Projected Distribution of Users of O. T. C. Tranquilizers
Upper/Upper Middle	17%	30%
Middle	70%	66%
Lower	13%	4%

The use of the nonprescription tranquilizers *does* appear to be associated more with whites than blacks.

Major Races	Projected Distribution of the General Population	Projected Distribution of Users of O. T. C. Tranquilizers
White	89%	97%
Black	10%	2%
All Other	1%	1%

Our survey data indicate the major consumers of these nonprescription tranquilizers are housewives and employed females.

Labor Force Categories	Approximate Distribution of the Population	Distribution of Users of O. T. C. Tranquilizers
Females	(54%)	(70%)
Students	7%	16%
Employed	21%	24%
Unemployed/ N. I. L. F.	26%	30%
Males	(46%)	(30%)
Students	8%	6%
Employed	36%	22%
Unemployed/ N. I. L. F.	2%	2%

In summary, the consumption of over-the-counter tranquilizers is indeed widespread throughout our population. One out of every ten persons over age 13 has taken them at one time or another with probably a half million people using them every week. The major consumers of these drugs appear to be females, primarily housewives and employed females. The use of these non-prescription tranquilizers appear to be disproportionately consumed by the upper level socioeconomic groups and by whites.

Summary and Comments

The use of nonprescription sedating, tranquilizing, and stimulating medications has been shown to be widespread. For example, within the population above the age of 13, some 12% are believed to have used the sedatives, 10% have used the tranquilizers, and 11% have used the stimulants. Translated to projected numbers of people, the following involvements were identified.

Persons Who Used These Drugs

Drug Class	Ever Used	Used Last Six Months	Used Last Week
1. Sleep Inducers	18,000,000	4,000,000	1,000,000
2. Stimulants	16,000,000	3,000,000	500,000
3. Tranquilizers	15,000,000	2,500,000	500,000

With regard to characterizing the users of these drugs white middle class and above females, normally housewives, who are over the age of 35 are the major consumers of the sleep inducers and their counterparts below the age of 35 are the major consumers of the tranquilizers. White middle class and above males under age 35 are the major consumers of the stimulants.

Overrepresentations Among Recent Users

	Sex	Age Groups	Socioeconomic Status	Race	Employment Status
Sedatives	Females	50 +	None	None	Unemployed N.I.L.F.
Stimulants	Males	-35	None	None	Students Employed
Tran- quilizers	Females	-35	Upper Upper Middle	Whites	Students Unemployed N.I.L.F.

Proprietary medicines are estimated to cost about 64 cents per week for a family of four, representing some *25%* of the total medicine market.[4] Without question, mass media advertizing creates and sustains this market.

Not unexpectedly, our surveys have documented the high incidence of over-the-counter drug use among females. In two of the three drug groups investigated, females were disproportionately overrepresented. For example, while females account for some 54% of the base population, they also represent 62% of the recent users of sleep inducers, and 70% of the recent users of tranquilizers. We have no recourse but to believe a major part of this overrepresentation can be explained by the focus of mass media advertising of over-the-counter drugs.

During 1971, Richard Heffner Associates, Inc. of New York City examined over-the-counter television commercials at the request of the National Commission on Marijuana and Drug Abuse.[5] Their data indicated that some 13% of the *network* commercials were over-the-counter drug oriented and that females, especially housewives, were seemingly a major target audience of

[4]Paul Warnke, Daniel O'Keefe, and Ari Kiev, "The Proprietary Association Replies to the Critics," *Journal of Drug Issues,* 4 (Summer 1974), pp. 217-222.

[5]Richard Heffner Associates, Inc., "Over-the-Counter Drug Commercials: Network Television, Spring, 1971," pp. 669-697, in "Drug Use in America: Problems in Perspective. The Technical Papers of the Second Report of the National Commission on Marijuana and Drug Abuse; Volume II: Social Responses to Drug Use" (Washington, D.C.: U.S. Government Printing Office, 1973).

the drug industry's efforts. More than half of the drug advertisements, for example, occurred in daytime television and 44% appeared in women-oriented daytime serials and quiz and audience participation shows. More specifically, because of the predominance of women-oriented programs during the noon to mid-afternoon time slot, proportionately more drug commercials appeared during those hours on a 5-day week basis than during the 3-1/2-hour nightly prime time. Furthermore, in commercials where there was a drug product *purchaser,* a female was the purchaser in 83% of the advertisements. In those commercials where there was a drug product *user,* disproportionately more of these users were females than males.

Our survey data support other aspects of how drug manufacturers focus toward specific target audiences. For example, in most of the television commercials, the purported users and purchasers in more than 90% of the cases were members of the white middle or upper class. This is indeed the case with the majority of our recent users. Based on the identifiable ages of the users and purchasers in the commercials, sleeping medications were targeted at persons 35 years and over -- the majority of the recent users in our surveys are age 35 and over.

It would be most difficult to *determine* the full impact of the subliminal influences of mass media promotions. It is not too difficult to speculate as to what happens when you focus the advertising of such chemical coping medications as Cope, Compoz, Nytol, Sleepeze, etc., toward a specific group of people on a high frequency continuous basis at a specific time when only that group of people are at risk for exposure to the advertising.

PART III

Alcohol

X

Brief
History
of
Alcohol

Introduction

Man's desire to temporarily alter or change the
reality in which he operates is perhaps one of the
oldest and most pervasive of his wishes. In order to
accomplish it he has, at various times and in various
places, subjected his body to beatings and mutilation,
starvation and sensory deprivation; he has focused his
mind solely on a single object; or let his consciousness
expand without direction searching for a transcendental
state; and he has often taken a more direct route...the
alteration of his mood and his ability to perceive and
act upon the world outside of him by the utilization
of drugs. Of these substances, the one that has probably
been used by more of the earth's peoples in more places
and times is the by-product of a simple organism's
conversion of sugar and water into energy - beverage
alcohol or ethanol. Last year almost 70% of America's
population -- more than 100 million persons -- experienced, to some degree, the effects of alcohol.

Alcohol: A Brief History

Like many of his most significant inventions, man's discovery of alcohol probably occurred during the stone age. Someone left some berries or grapes in a vessel for a few days. When he returned, airborne yeasts had already begun fermenting the mixture. The result, undoubtedly, provoked more interest than the original fruit. One might surmise that the discoverer then applied his creativity to improving his invention. Man soon learned that it was possible and desirable to cultivate plants and domesticate certain animals, instead of just simply hunting for and gathering his food. These primitive agriculturalists discovered ways of transforming the starch of their grains, which yeasts cannot metabolize, into fermentable sugar. As is still done in many parts of the world today, the grain was chewed, but not swallowed, since the enzyme responsible for this transformation is found naturally in saliva, and then it expectorated into a prepared mash. In this way beer came into being. Man quickly discovered that not only fruits, berries, and grains could be used to produce alcohol...leaves, tubers, flowers, cacti, milk, and even honey could be fermented.

These early concoctions (roughly designated as wines or beers) though were limited in their alcoholic strength. As the yeasts metabolize the sugar and water, carbon dioxide (which is what makes bread rise or gives beer a head) and alcohol are released as by-broducts. When, however, the alcoholic content of the mixture achieves a proportion of 14% the yeasts are rendered inactive (i.e., killed) and fermentation stops entirely. In addition to the limitation imposed by the biology of the yeasts, the alcoholic content was affected by the producer as well. Whether he was able to assure that his fermentation mixture contained enough sugar to allow the yeast to produce all the alcohol, or, even whether he was willing to allow the yeasts the time necessary to complete the fermentation process, all would have a crucial bearing on the potency of his product. It was not until the close of the Middle Ages, however, that Western man was to have drinks with an alcoholic content of more than 14%. In Europe during this time someone discovered that distilling, i.e., boiling off and isolating the more volatile alcohol from the other fluids, makes possible a considerably more potent beverage. Beverages then almost quadrupled in potency, achieving an alcoholic content of 50% or more. Now a third class of beverages -- spirits -- was made universally available.

What is this drug which has been called by some the "water of life" -- *aqua vitae,* in scholastic Latin -- or ambrosia -- the nectar of the gods -- and "the corruptor of youth" and the "the devils' own brew" by others? Ethyl alcohol or ethanol (whose chemical formula is C_2H_5OH) is a clear, colorless liquid with little odor but a powerful burning taste. Ethanol is just one of many alcohols such as methyl (wood) and isopropyl (rubbing) alcohol. All others have toxic effects and cannot be readily metabolized by the body; these properties making them entirely unsuitable for consumption.

In addition to ethanol and water, alcoholic beverages generally contain minute amounts of substances referred to as congeners. Many of these chemicals are important to the flavor and aroma of the beverage. Brandy, for example, is relatively rich in these congeners while vodka contains relatively few. There is some evidence suggesting that the after-effects of excessive drinking, i.e., the hangover, are related to the presence of these congeners. The postintoxication effects will be greater after consuming drinks righer in congeners.

As we all know, alcoholic beverages differ in strength. Beer generally has an alcoholic content of 5%, malt liquors are slightly higher. Natural wine varies in alcoholic content between 6% and 14%. Fortified wines contain between 17% and 20% alcohol. Hard liquor or spirits contain approximately 40% ethanol. The designation of "proof" originated centuries ago as a test for the potency of a beverage. If gun powder saturated with alcohol exploded upon ignition, this was taken as "proof" that the liquor was more than half pure alcohol. In the United States proof is calculated as being twice the percentage of ethanol by unit volume of beverage (thus an 86 proof Scotch is 43% alcohol).

It is important to understand that even though the relative strengths of the beverages differ, one consumes essentially the same amount of ethanol in the standard portions of the drink. In other words, one consumes the same quantity of absolute alcohol if he drinks either a 12-ounce bottle of beer, a three- to four-ounce glass of wine, or a cocktail made with one and one-half ounces i.e., one shot) of distilled spirits.

XI

Effects
of
Alcohol

Some Physical Effects

Unlike most other foodstuffs alcohol is absorbed
directly into the blood stream without digestion. A
small amount passes directly through the stomach
lining itself; most, however, progresses on to the
small intestine where it is almost entirely absorbed.
Although one may be experiencing a burning sensation
or diffuse warmth directly following a drink, these
sensations are the results of the irritating effect
that alcohol has on the tissues of the mouth, esophagus
(food-tube), and stomach. Alcohol does not become intoxicating until the blood carrying it reaches the
brain. The rapidity with which this occurs is in large
measure determined by the condition of the stomach.
An empty stomach will facilitate the absorption of the
alcohol while a full stomach will retard it. To some
degree the type of beverage involved has an effect on
absorption, as well. Beer, for example, contains food
substances which tend to retard this absorption. Drinks
which are noticeably carbonated -- such as champagne --
seem to "quickly go to one's head," since the carbon

dioxide facilitates the passage of alcohol from the
stomach to the small intestine.

Alcohol is held in the tissues of the body before
it is broken down (i.e., oxidized) like any other food
substance. The body oxidizes alcohol at a steady rate,
with the individual being able to exercise very little
control over this process. Therefore, an average sized
man (ca. 160 lbs.) drinking three-fourths of an ounce
of distilled spirits every hour could consume more than
a pint in a 24-hour period and not experience any marked
intoxication. If the same quantity was consumed over
a few hours, however, the person would be very drunk.
Today much research is directed at finding an "antidote"
for alcohol. In other words a chemical that would either
breakdown the alcohol itself, or alleviate the body's
metabolic process. Although we have several promising
leads, no such drug appears to be imminent. The belief
that black coffee (i.e., caffeine) is an antidote is
essentially without fact. What the caffeine does do,
however, is to stimulate the drinker -- the intoxicated
person is still "drunk" although he may, after several
cups of black coffee, be more awake.

Ethanol is broken down (metabolized) in the liver.
In experiments, animals have had their livers removed,
and then were given ethyl alcohol. The alcohol remained,
much like wood (methyl) alcohol, in their bodies without being fully metabolized and demonstrated the toxic
effects -- such as nerve damage -- brought on by the
unpotable alcohols. The liver is vital because this is
the organ containing the enzymes necessary for the
metabolism of the substance. In the liver, the alcohol
combines with the enzyme(s) and is transformed into
acetaldehyde. This acetaldehyde is much more toxic
than alcohol. However, as soon as it formed, other

bodily processes activate to change (i.e., oxidize) it
into acetic acid (like found in vinegar) an innocuous
substance. The ascetic acid is then further broken down
into carbon dioxide and water. Interestingly, one of
the medical controls for the treatment of alcoholism
employs the metabolic process itself. Antabuse (disul-
firam) is a chemical which prohibits the body from
converting acetaldehyde to ascetic acid. Alone, Antabuse has little effect on the individual; and the
patient is given a daily dose of it. If any alcohol,
however, is drunk the acetaldehyde produced collects
quickly much to the very great discomfort of the individual.

Alcohol, like other food stuffs, does have some
nutritional value. Undoubtedly the primitive brews and
concoctions were richer in nutritional value, especially
vitamins and minerals than the highly refined beverages
we have available today. Alcohol itself is a rich
source of calories which the body can convert into
energy and heat. An ounce of whiskey provides approximately 75 calories -- or the equivalent of a potato, an
ear of corn, a slice of dark bread, or a serving of
spaghetti. If one consumes mixed drinks, the caloric
content often doubles due to the sweetness in the mixer.
These extra calories are, of course, fattening provided
the drinker does not reduce his intake of other foods.
Beverages such as beer contain additional food value
in the form of carbohydrates as well. With the new
interest in figure control and weight reduction, however, brewers are attempting to even remove these. A
low calorie "beer" is now on the market.

The fact that alcohol provides sufficient calories
for the individual to subsist on provides an additional
health hazard. Many heavy drinkers, for example, express

a preference to "drink their meals." While alcohol
does provide these calories, other nutrients, such as
proteins, vitamins, and minerals vital to health and
continued well being, are entirely lacking. These
heavy drinkers often suffer from chronic malnutrition
and deficiency diseases.

Short-Term Effects

Alcohol exerts its most profound effects on the brain.
Interestingly, the observable behavior produced by
drinking is as much a result of the social situation
the individual drinks in, his mood, and his expectations
about what the drinking will do to or for him as it is
the actual quantity of alcohol consumed. On two different occasions, for example, drinking the identical
quantity and type of beverage, the individual might
experience euphoria or depression; or, he may feel full
of energy or simply wish to sleep; or, a drink found
initially stimulating will encourage sleep. Pharmacologically, alcohol is a central nervous system depressant drug. Little is known about the operation of
the specific mechanisms, but some research has suggested
that alcohol acts most directly on those portions of
the brain which control sleep and wakefulness.

Conventionally, the amount of alcohol within a
person can be described by his Blood Alcohol Content
(B.A.C.). This measures the proportion of alcohol that
might be found within an individual's bloodstream;
typically it is measured by the amount of alcohol ex-
haled as the blood is oxygenated through the lungs by
a machine called a breathalyzer. Although, as we men-
tioned, the effects vary by both drinking situation
and the experience that the drinker has had, we can in
a rather rough way expect to see some of the following
occur. After two or three drinks, in a short period of

time, a man of average size (160 lbs.) will begin to feel the effects of the drug. There may be a feeling of exhilaration; of being on the top of the world; a freeing of inhibitions and the loosening of one's tongue; people seem more likely to be willing to act on impulse while caution and judgment often take a second place to bravado. Such a person would have an approximate B.A.C. of 0.05%.

If our subject drinks another three drinks in a short period, his B.A.C. will elevate to around 0.1%. Now, besides affecting some of the higher centers of thought and judgment located in the cerebral cortex, the alcohol is beginning to act on some of the lower (more basic) motor areas of the brain. By law in most states, the subject now would be judged incapable of operating a motor vehicle, and if caught doing so would be charged with "driving under the influence." Behaviorally such a person would have some difficulty walking, appearing to lurch somewhat; there would be noticeable decline in activities requiring fine hand-eye coordination; and a slurring of speech.

At higher concentrations of alcohol from 0.2% and up (resulting from the consumption of at least 10 ounces of spirits) more of the central nervous system is affected. The drinker has difficulty coordinating even his simplest movements and needs assistance to even walk or undress. His emotions appear very unstable and he may change from rage to tears and then back again in a very few moments. At 0.4% to 0.5% alcohol depresses enough of the central nervous system that the drinker lapses into a coma and at concentrations of 0.7% and above the most basic centers of the brain -- those that affect respiration and heartbeat are so suppressed that death is a likely result. (Death solely by "alcohol overdose" is relatively rare, however, because one lapses into unconsciousness before the critical level is reached.)

Other Effects

While the most immediate and profound effects of alcohol are in the central nervous system, other organs are affected as well. Alcohol stimulates the flow of gastric juices in the stomach, giving one the sensation of hunger, this might partially explain the popularity of a cocktail before dinner. It is for this reason, as well, that persons suffering from stomach ulcers are enjoined from drinking. The sexual stimulation that one seems to receive from alcohol does not occur because of excitation of the responsible glands. Instead, it occurs through the lessening of inhibitions. However, while it may increase desire, alcohol in sufficient quantity reduces the ability to perform. For males erection and ejaculation become increasingly more difficult as the B.A.C. increases and for females it becomes increasingly more difficult to achieve orgasm. Recent research has suggested, as well, that chronic alcoholic men often sustain damage to the central nervous system that makes normal sexual performance very difficult or even impossible. Unfortunately, these effects often persist even after a prolonged period of abstinence.

For the normal person in good health a small amount of alcohol -- even taken on a daily basis -- will do no harm. It is only with the sustained drinking of larger quantities of alcohol that we can expect to see alcohol-related problems appearing. The liver of one who abuses alcohol is marked by fatty deposits and scar tissue, giving it a swollen appearance, and a decline in the number of healthy cells. Cirrhosis of the

liver may develop after several years of heavy drinking
and can lead to death. While alcohol is the major of-
fender in this condition, poor diet and poor living
situations contribute significantly.

Heart disease is more prevalent among heavy drinkers
than in the general population. Gastrointestinal disorders as well as cancers of the mouth, esophagus, and
stomach are somewhat more prevalent among heavy drinkers
than the general population.

The most serious threat to the heavy drinker, however, is the possibility of addiction to alcohol or
alcohol dependence. Addiction to alcohol can and does
occur and the severe withdrawal symptoms that occur on
the sudden cessation or drastic decrease in consumption
can be life threatening -- considerably more so than
the withdrawal symptoms appearing during opiate withdrawal.

The death rates among alcohol-dependent persons are
much higher than those in the general population. The
usual indicators of mental health, such as suicide rates,
admissions to mental hospitals, and the like, clearly
suggest that this population is not a healthy one.
Alcohol, man's oldest domesticated drug, is also one
of his greatest enemies. In America we estimate that
there are somewhere around five million alcoholics and
double that proportion of "problem drinkers" many of
whom are early stage alcoholics. Some investigators
have estimated that at least one-half of our fatal
automobile accidents have an alcohol-impaired driver
involved. Research has suggested that in a disturbing
large proportion of violent crimes either perpetrator,
victim, or both had been drinking. It is clear that we
are willing to pay a large price for this chemical com-
fort. Perhaps now we should turn our attention to the
use of alcohol by Americans today.

XII

Alcohol
Use
and
Abuse

Patterns of Use

Since so many people use alcohol, in so many different contexts and in so many different contexts and in so many different ways, it makes little sinse to simply classify people as "drinkers" or nondrinkers." Also, although people may be daily or weekly users, their consumption at each drinking occurrence may be noticeably different. In order to realistically measure the varying consumption patterns, all three dimensions of drinking behavior -- quantity, frequency, and variability -- must be considered. This was done and each element was combined so that an index or measure of drinking could be established. Through the use of this index we were able to classify the population into five groups, each representing their drinking pattern. These groups are:

> I. ABSTAINERS -- Those persons who drink no alcoholic beverages as often as once a year.

> II. INFREQUENT DRINKERS -- Persons who drink at least once a year but less than once a month.

III. LIGHT DRINKERS -- Persons who
always limit their intake to
one or two drinks.

IV. MODERATE DRINKERS -- Are persons
who characteristically drink
several times during the month
but almost always limit their
consumption to three or four
drinks on each occasion.

V. HEAVY DRINKERS -- Are persons
who typically drink every day
and often consume five or six
drinks at each incident or
several drinks during the day.

The index is similar to the ones that have been used
in state and national level surveys of drinking practices. As such, many of our findings can be meaningful
compared to previous research.

Prevalence of Use

"Prevalence" is a measure of the extent of some
behavior within a general population; it does not
necessarily mean that people are currently doing some-
thing, rather that they have at least one time, experienced it. The data on prevalence demonstrate that
an overwhelming majority of Americans, above the age
of 13, have had at least some experience with alcohol.
More than four-fifths of our population -- close to
125 million persons have drunk alcohol. Slightly less
than 15% of the (projected to be almost 23 million
persons) persons sampled, although reporting drinking
in the past, claim current i.e., in the last year)
abstinence. Of these current nondrinkers most report
that their usage in the past occurred only on rare or
infrequent occasions. A small proportion of these
former drinkers claimed they quit because of a drinking
problem, or the fear of developing one. The data concerning how they quit tend to be inconclusive: some

received special help in doing so, from a physician or
Alcoholics Anonymous, for example, and some did not.
This is not to say, of course, that people "in trouble"
can always help themselves, but that there may be re-
sources that we have not come to recognize yet the
future, hopefully, will see this question fully explored.

Patterns and Extent of Drinking

While roughly one-third of America's population,
above the age of 13, claim abstinence -- that is, no
drinking in the year preceding their interview -- we
project that the remaining two-thirds (68% or more than
100 million persons) drank some alcohol last year.
Approximately half of these are estimated to be "regular
drinkers"; that is, they drink alcohol at least once a
month. The remaining portion are "infrequent drinkers"
who drank at least once last year, but less frequently
than once a month. Looking at the entire population once
again, our classification suggests the following projections:

12% are Heavy Drinkers

11% are Moderate Drinkers

23% are Light Drinkers

The data suggest that the great majority of regular
drinkers demonstrate drinking patterns which, in themselves, carry little or a minimal probability of
alcohol-related problems. Two things should be noted,
however. The first is that, as of yet, no index capable
of reliability predicting who will ultimately "get

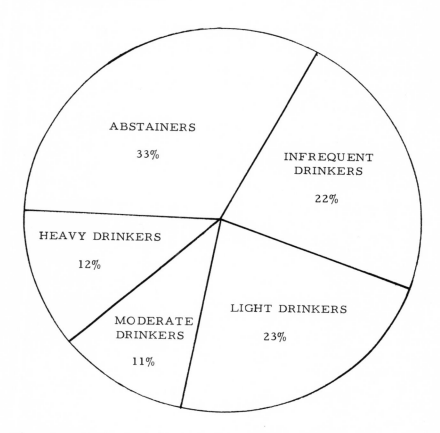

Fig. 1. Projected distribution of alcohol usage patterns.

into trouble" with or because of alcohol has been de-
veloped. Second is that the end result of drinking is
as much "situational" as it is pharmacological. Whether
a drinker will actually ever experience any problems
because of his drinking may have as much to do with his
social class, employment situation, and even religion,
as his consumption levels. Thus far, we know that people
do get into trouble with drinking and we also know that
certain situations and certain ethnic and social groups
seem to have a higher potential for problems than others.

However, we have not been able to put the two together
into any type of predictive statement. Much research
is progressing along these lines, and hopefully, we
will soon be able to better understand the occurrence
of problem drinking.

Regular Drinkers: Demographic and Social Characteristics

What does the drinking half of the nation's population look like? Are these people with little to do and
much time on their hands? Or are they, as we seem to
feel, a rather good cross section of America's people?

Sex. Of those who drink regularly most are
males.

Sex	Percent of Regular Drinkers	Percent Representation in General Population Above Age 13
Male	61%	46%
Female	39%	54%

We have reason to believe, however, that the proportion
of women in the nation's population of regular drinkers
is rising slowly but steadily. We suspect that as women
become increasingly more liberated and integrated into
the occupational structure of this country their drinking
behavior will become increasingly more like men's. It
is not at all unreasonable to expect more working women
will turn to the comforting cocktail at the end of an
arduous day. Too, sex roles are both losing some of their
traditional authority as well as depolarizing. Both of
these can be expected to have a significant impact on
drinking behavior. Today, in most places a woman can
drink, as well as smoke in public, fearing for neither
her reputation nor self-image. Contributing to this
trend is probably the fact that, as some researchers

have suggested, the alcoholic beverage industry has recognized the importance of this newly emerging feminine market and are gearing both their products and advertising to it.

Sex and age. Of the five age groups, or cohorts, our findings suggest that in each of the male cohorts -- excluding adolescents -- at least half are regular drinkers. While we never quite achieve this representation among females the data suggest that the distribution -- or the shape of the curves -- is quite similar between the sexes. Drinking seems to peak during those stages-of-life designated as "early adulthood" and "adulthood" (roughly between the ages of 18 and 34). The female peak expectedly occurs several years earlier than the males. A number of factors might be in operation here. One might suggest that the years between 18 and 24 are perhaps the most socially active of a young woman's life. Too, these are the years when most people go to college. Since college is a time of experimentation, it is not as all unreasonable to assume that alcohol may be one of the things to be experimented with and subsequently discontinued when the individual's social milieu changes. For young men, the picture is at once similar and yet different. The peak of their drinking curve occurs during the "early adulthood" stage. This is the time that many young men are most active. Many are just beginning in careers and find that socializing and entertaining plays an important role in business. Many of these ambitious young men are beginning to feel the pressures of career strivings. The change in role from "student" to "business man" or "professional" carries with it, for some, a measure of anxiety. Many report that a drink or two at the end of the day makes it easier for them to relax, to make the

necessary change-over from hard-driving, ambitious
young executives to husbands and fathers. Many of these
young people find that because of their extremely mobile
life styles it is impossible to settle in one place for
very long and friends are left almost as soon as they
are made. Alcohol, they have found, helps "take some of

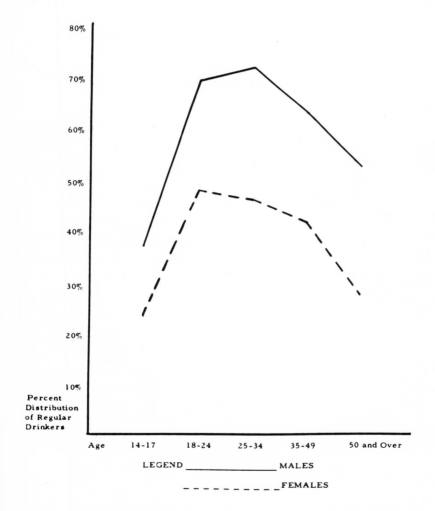

Fig. 2. Regular drinkers -- sex and age by cohort.

the edges off things" and makes it considerably easier
for people to relate to (probably on just a superficial
level) each other.

While these data do demonstrate a rather high climb
in these early, intensely productive years, one can
easily observe the drop in prevalence as the cohorts
age. Factors such as a constricting social life (here
we are referring, for example, to attending fewer
parties), more job security, fewer role changes, and in
latter years a considerably smaller income all contribute to the declining representation of drinkers in
the older cohorts.

> $\times$ *Race or Ethnicity*. The racial/ethnic compo-
sition of the nation's regular drinkers is not strik-
ingly different than base line projections mady by the
1970 census.

Racial Distribution of Regular Drinkers

Major Races	Percent (Projected) Regular Drinkers	Percent (Projected) General Population
White	85%	89%
Black	12%	10%
Other	3%	1%

Although regular drinking is proportional to the total
population distribution, we would suspect that the
social organization of drinking behavior differs somewhat from racial group to racial group. We would further
suspect that social class differences figure even more
prominently into the determination of the drinking
patterns. And, within both the race and class (or
status division) the social organization of the drinking behavior is strongly influenced by other social

characteristics such as upbrining, parent's nativity,
and religious orientation, just to mention a few.

X   *Social Class.* The distribution of regular
drinkers within the population points to a preponderance
of middle class persons. We propose that the social
status distribution of the nation's regular drinkers
could be projected as follows:

Socioeconomic Class	Projected Distribution of the General Population	Projected Distribution of Regular Drinkers
Upper/Upper Middle	17%	19%
Middle	70%	69%
Lower	13%	12%

Measures of social class or status include education,
income, residential area -- in short all the ways that
we have for differentiating people. If we wish to be
somewhat more precise we can see that our population
can be along other variables as well.

X   *Occupation.* A man's occupation often tells
much about him. It generally defines the company he
keeps, the style and manner in which he lives, and the
way he spends the bulk of his time. We propose that the
occupational distribution of the county's regular
drinkers could be projected as follows:

Occupational Distribution (Projected) of the United State's Regular Drinkers *

Occupational Group	Representation in General Population	Proportion of Regular Drinkers
Professionals, Technical, Managers	14%	16%
White Collar, Clerical	10%	5%
Skilled, Semi-Skilled	17%	21%
Unskilled	3%	7%

* "Other" and "No Data" categories have been excluded.

There are two trends worthy of notice. Previous research has suggested, and our studies are in general agreement, that as one's educational and/or social class level elevates there is more of a likelihood that he will drink. What we have seen, however, is that while the general incidence of alcoholic use does demonstrate an increase, the intensity of drinking appears to be somewhat less in these higher status groups. This will become clearer as we discuss heavy drinking and some of the social cost and liabilities incurred through alcohol use. The nation's population will now be used as a base line with which to compare other drinking conditions and groups that have experienced alcohol-related problems.

While we have highlighted those groups that are commonly designated as "gainfully employed," some mention should be made of the drinking practices of persons not in the labor force, as well. Some special note should be made concerning the representation of high school students within the nation's population of regular drinkers. The use of alcohol, unless it

Distribution (Projected) of Regular Drinkers - Non-Gainfully
Employed Categories

Category	Representation in General Population	Proportion of Regular Drinkers
Male High School Students	5%	4%
Female High School Students	5%	2%
Male College Students	3%	3%
Female College Students	2%	2%
Housewives	24%	16%

occurs in the home, by this group is of questionable
legality at best. Data, although not entirely con-
clusive at this time, are beginning to suggest that
use of alcohol by the nation's adolescents is on the
increase. Moreover, for many adolescents alcohol is
taken in their search for new and better highs along
with an increasingly wide variety of other psychoactive
chemicals (marijuana, nonbarbiturate sedatives, and
powerful analgesics). There is little question that
such indiscriminate drug usage can only be deleterious
to one's health. And in the case of the adolescents,
we have no way of knowing what effect this kind of prolonged poly-drug abuse will have on subsequent psycho-
social adjustment.

Heavy Drinkers -- Their Profile

While some people mistakenly equate heavy alcohol
use with "alcoholism" and "heavy drinkers" with
"alcoholics," such is not the case. We can, however,
be reasonably secure in suggesting that heavy drinkers

probably "enjoy" the effects of alcohol more than their lighter-drinking counterparts; or, that alcohol "does more" for these people and, therefore, its effects are more consistently pursued. The reasons for drinking. of course, are multitudinous: to relax, to get high, to forget, to overcome shyness -- essentially, all-things-to-all-people. The heavy user, though, has come to rely more on this drug, ethanol, to give him what he thinks he needs. He depends more on his chemical "assistant" rather than on himself or his fellows to help him out in times of trouble or uncertainty. Unfortunately, the sword is a double-edged one. As useful as it may be, any drug exacts a price. While the drug invariably begins as an assistant, it may quickly be transformed into the master. This is, of course, the most radical price one can pay, other costs -- some measurable monetarily and some not -- can be accrued.

For rather obvious reasons, heavy drinkers demonstrate the greatest probability for alcohol related problems. Those who persist in a pattern of heavy drinking over the course of years can ultimately expect to have to "pay the price." while only a very few will become so dysfunctional that they will find their way onto the nation's skid rows, many will suffer from alcohol-connected health problems and perhaps experience a measure of psychological and/or social impairment. The findings to be presented below relate only to persons currently living in households. Skid-row or homeless-type drinkers as well as persons with problems so severe as to require institutionalization have *not* been included in this profile.

Sex and Age. While males tend to be over-represented (i.e., exceed their proportion in the universe) in the nation's population of regular drinkers, this preponderance of males is even greater among those who drink heavily.

Sex Distribution of Heavy Drinkers Compared to Regular Drinkers and Base Population

	Percent General Population	Percent Moderate and Light Drinkers	Percent Heavy Drinkers
Males	46%	55%	77%
Females	54%	45%	23%

When presented like this, the differences become striking. While the general use of alcohol is becoming increasingly desexualized, the heavy drinking pattern, however, still retains the strong sexual polarity. As one might expect, certain areas of the country are beginning to report that some noticeable inroads are being made by women into the population of heavy drinkers. We suspect that the future will witness a steady acceleration of this trend as the social distance separating women and men gradually shrinks.

The age distribution of the nation's population of heavy drinkers is somewhat different than the universe of regular drinkers. Among males, the early and adulthood years sees the greatest incidence of heavy drinking. The shape of the curves is interesting: regular drinking in the population appears to peak in the adulthood years, while heavy drinking peaks in the early adulthood period. Although the shape is somewhat different, the distribution of regular and heavy drinking males in each age group in the nation's population is roughly similar. This similarity between regular and heavy drinkers is not to be found in the female groups. While the distribution of female regular drinkers is quite similar in appearance to the male distributions, the distribution of female heavy drinkers, when con-

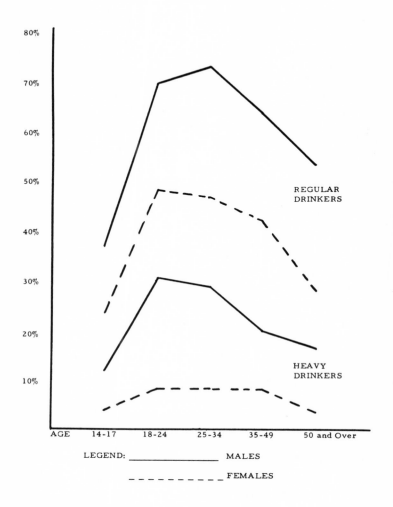

Fig. 3.   Sex and age by cohort.

sidered by age group, is more reminiscent of a plateau.
The proportion of heavy drinkers in each age group is
similar all through the adult years, i.e., from 18 to
49, and then declines.

These data lead to some interesting speculations.
As we have suggested earlier, the proportion of heavy

drinking males by age group is noticeably greater than among females. We suspect that alcohol is used by many of them to deal with much of the anxiety generated through social living. The societal emphasis on "working-hard-and-playing-hard" would encourage the heavy use of alcohol as both euphoriant and social lubricant. As one approaches the middle years, though, some of these pressures decrease and the incidence of all drinking drops sharply. The proportion of heavy drinkers among each female group, recall, is noticeably smaller than among males. The plateau, however, suggests that the pattern has a good deal more resiliency among females than among males. Heavy drinking in these adult female cohorts appears to be fairly stable.

Race and Ethnicity. These findings suggest that although minority groups tend not to be overrepresented in their use of alcohol, those who do drink tend to drink more. *The incidence of heavy drinking is noticeably higher among minority groups*. Notice the steep decline in the proportion of whites and the sharp increase in the proportions of all minority groups. The abuse of this most accessible of the psychoactive chemicals is perhaps one coping response to the problems created by the economic and social deprivation these groups experience.

Social Class. As in the case above, alcohol may be used by some to cope with the stresses and tensions coming from an inferior social and economic situation. Our surveys indicate that heavy drinking is somewhat less prevalent among society's upper strata and conversely more common among its lower strata. Seen in terms of what we know about drinking behavior...while the use of alcohol tends to enjoy a positive relationship to social class, the heavy use of alcohol enjoys

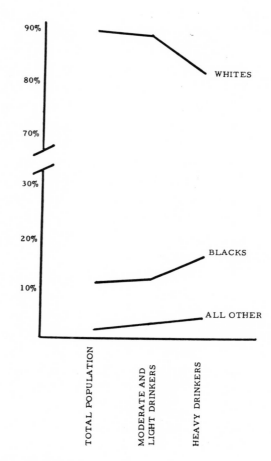

Fig. 4.   Drinking pattern by race.

a negative or inverse relationship with social class.

  Occupation. When the representation of heavy
to moderate and light drinkers is considered within
occupational groups, the findings are rather clear.
Heavy drinkers are most prominently represented in the
trades; almost half of the heavy drinkers surveyed are
employed as either skilled, semi-skilled, or unskilled
workers. In the other occupational categories the pro-

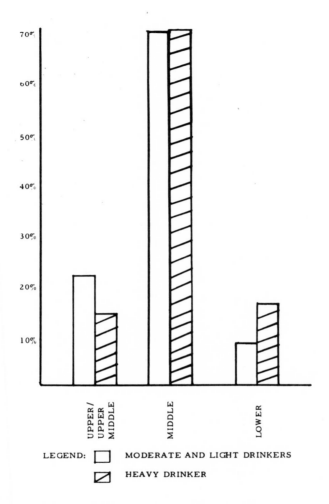

Fig. 5.   Drinking pattern by social class.

portion of moderate and light drinkers outweight the
heavy users.

The Drinking Situation

   Alcohol is used in a wide variety of social contexts.
Ritualistically, Jews have always used wine in the
sanctification of the Sabbath and other holidays. For

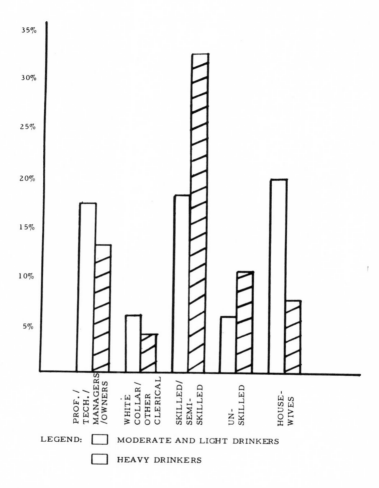

Fig. 6.   Employment status characteristics and drinking pattern.

many Mediterranean groups, alcohol in the form of wine is seen as a food and most drinking occurs at mealtimes. Ceremonially, alcohol in many different forms is used to celebrate an occurrence, seal a contract, or denote good fellowship. Convivially, the consumption of alcohol becomes a part of many social gatherings or the focus

of a night's activity. "making-the-rounds" by visiting
a succession of drinking establishments.

In our surveys, we have not fully explored all the
social contexts in which drinking normally occurs and
the meanings and definitions that the participants in-
vest in them. What we have done is to abstract two of
the major elements -- the place and the involvement of
other people in the drinking situation.

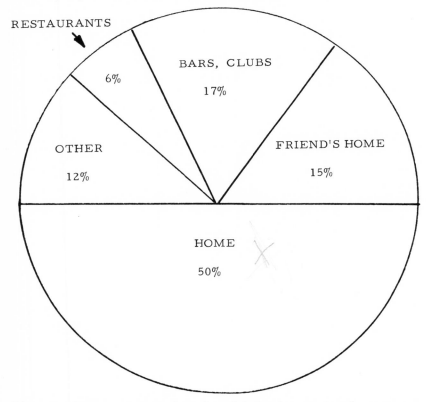

Fig. 7. Place or setting in which the respondent most
often does his drinking.

Place. As illustrated, for most of our respondents, the home is the major locus of his drinking
activity. Home's of friends account for approximately

another 15% of the total, placing the majority of
drinking behavior in a convivial or domestic context.
In addition to the home, bars or clubs are the next
most important *situs* of drinking.

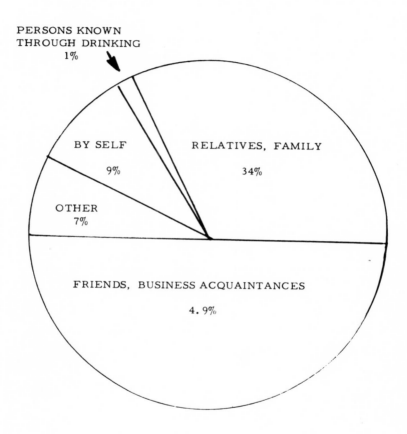

Fig. 8.   Projected distribution of person or persons
with whom the respondent most often does his drinking.

Our surveys clearly indicate an overwhelming majority
of respondents do their drinking in a business or convivial setting. A small proportion, approximately 10%
(projected to be in excess of 15 million people) report

that they do most of their drinking alone or with people
known solely through drinking.

Solitary Drinking. What about this minority...
how do they compare to the larger universe of regular
drinkers? Of the many drinking patterns, solitary drinking has long been recognized as one of the most problematic. It can imply, for example, that the effects of
the alcohol have become more important than the setting
or the social context of the drinking incident; that
the person is willing to endanger social ties by violat-
ing his group's norms and drinking. It can imply, as
well, that the individuals behavior has deteriorated
beyond the base limit necessary to sustain social inter-
action. Or it may imply a clear pattern of self-medication where the individual is drinking to cope with life
problems such as loneliness, ennui, or depression.

These solitary drinkers are overwhelmingly male and
tend to be older...almost 85% of the respondents were
male, this represents a 20% increase in the proportion
of males found in the regular drinkers. These solitary
drinkers are older, as well. Compare the following table.

Age	General Population	Regular Drinkers	Solitary Drinkers
14-17	10%	7%	1%
18-24	16%	19%	7%
25-34	17%	18%	9%
35-49	25%	26%	31%
50 and above	32%	29%	52%

More than three-fourths are in the mature adult age
group and more slightly over half are 50 years old or
older.

These solitary drinkers exhibit some very striking
differences in other social categories as well:

> Almost 30% of the men report being
> unemployed or not in the labor force
> while only 11% of the regularly
> drinking males report this status.
>
> Double the proportion (20% as against
> 10%) of lower class persons are to
> be found in the solitary drinking
> population as in the population of
> regular drinkers.
>
> The proportion of whites who are
> solitary drinkers declines noticeably
> while the proportion of non-whites
> increases dramatically.

These solitary drinkers might best be described as a "marginal population." "Marginality" is a sociological concept useful in describing someone who is outside of the main stream of society. The very impressive over-representation of poor people, minority group members, old people, and people without gainful employment all support that contention. We might speculate that for this and other similarly marginal populations alcohol is used as a primary coping mechanism -- a way to get through the day.

XIII

The
Toll
of
Alcoholism

The Costs

Although alcohol may help get through the day, and
perhaps the one after that as well, there are costs
that will ultimately have to be paid. A recent report
by the N.I.A.A.A. estimated that the highway death toll
in a single year is 28,000 persons; these accidents
annually injure a half-million people and involve more
than one billion dollars in property and medical damages.
Alcoholism and alcohol abuse cost the nation's economy
an estimated fifteen billion dollars a year. At least
$10 billion of this involves lost work time and the re-
mainder for health and welfare services for the alcoholic and those effected by his condition. Measured in
other terms as well, alcohol-related offenses account
for nearly one-third of the arrests made in the United
States; one can only surmise about the costs involved
and the diversion of law enforcement officers from
tasks deemed more valuable. All of these costs are
measured in terms of aggregates: dollars lost through
absenteeism, medical disbursements, and the lives lost
in automobile accidents. Yet these kinds of costs can

almost be seen as indirect. Below, we shall present
some of our findings concerning people who are actually
experiencing some measure of trouble with or because of
alcohol. Two different measures were employed in our
surveys. The first is an assessment of respondent reports that drinking is in some way beginning to be a
significant component in their lives: whether if no
longer able to do so they would really miss being able
to drink, or, whether they are worried or concerned
about their drinking. The second is more direct. Here
we assessed whether people have actually had alcohol
disrupt some area of their lives: either their family
lives, their job, or their legal standing.

       Involvement with Drinking. While not yet
necessarily dysfunctional the person who is to some
degree "involved" with drinking finds that alcohol is
playing a more significant part in his life. Drinking
is important to him -- either he is worried that he
might be drinking too much -- that he is in danger of
becoming an alcoholic; or even that he won't have a
steady enough supply of alcohol. Similarly the person
to whom drinking is so important that he would seriously
miss it if no longer able to do so, might be seen as
being an involved drinker.

    Approximately 16% of our survey respondents indicate
some degree of involvement with use/effects of alcohol.
Expectedly, males tend to predominate in this population.
Interestingly, the proportion of males who report that
they would miss drinking is noticeably greater than
among those who report being worried about drinking
(72% as against 63%). The age distributions in these
two areas further accentuate some of these differences.
Among those who report that they would miss drinking if
no longer able to do so, the distribution, by age cohort,

climbs noticeably until age 35 where it appears to level
out. These findings suggest that the use of alcohol, and
all that goes along with it, is well integrated into all
aspects of their lives. Among those who expressed a
measure of worry or concern about their drinking, however, the findings suggest a somewhat different distribution.

Age Distribution (Projected) of Involved Usage Variables: (Males Only)

Age	Regular Drinkers	Miss Drinking	Worried about Drinking
14-17	7%	5%	9%
18-24	19%	19%	26%
25-34	18%	22%	18%
35-49	27%	27%	30%
50 and above	31%	27%	18%

Among those worried about their drinking, rather
noticeable clustering occurs in the "young" and "mature"
adult age cohorts. One might speculate that it is at
these ages that some of life's most significant changes
and decisions occur. The young adult, confronted by new
responsibilities and added freedoms including, of course,
legal access to alcohol may find that this new freedom
makes him more than a little uncomfortable. Alcohol in
such a case, since members of this cohort are beginning
to drink more as they approach their adult patterns,
may be seen as particularly problematic. The mature
adult, however, may be responding to other of life's
crises. For the business and professional person this
may imply a leveling out of the career line, or the
actual perception that younger people may be advancing
beyond their position. Some may turn to alcohol for
relief of the anxiety accompanying these changes. While
they are able to temporarily cope with their anxiety

through chemical means, their change in drinking pattern
is apparently not without additional cost. These costs
occur now as anxiety about their drinking. Many quickly
find that in addition to their original problems the
added anxiety makes them feel even more trapped and
isolated.

Alcohol-Related Problems

While involved drinking primarily affects the drinker
and is mostly measured in subjective terms, social
problems, by definition, effect more than the individual.
For many reasons, we feel much more comfortable talking
about "problem drinkers" and "problem drinking" rather
than "alcoholism" and "alcoholics." Problem drinking
can be defined as the repetitive use of beverage alcohol
in such a manner that one's functioning within the
occupational, familial, and sociolegal spheres is
noticeably impaired. This conception is much more useful
since it stresses institutional and/or personal dys-
functionality, rather than any arbitrarily defined
drinking behavior or pattern. The respondent, himself,
was requested to make the determination by responding
to whether because of alcohol he experienced any difficulty in his family life, his job, or the law. Our
findings suggest that almost 14% of those who currently
drink or used to drink regularly in the past, have experienced some problem with or because of their drinking.
In terms of the actual distribution of problems the
following observations have been noted.

> We would project that this 14% involves
> almost 10 and a half million people who
> have had problems related to their
> drinking. The greatest majority of these
> have as yet only experienced this dis-
> ruption in a single area of their lives.
> A smaller proportion -- projected to be
> some 4% of the population or almost 3
> million persons report multiple alcohol
> related disruptions in their lives.

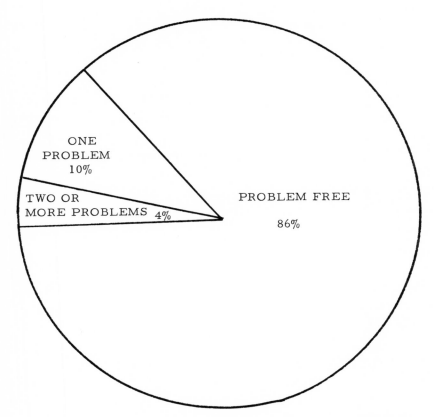

ONE
PROBLEM
10%

TWO OR
MORE PROBLEMS 4%

PROBLEM FREE

86%

Fig. 9. Distribution of alcohol-related social problems
among current and former regular/occasional drinkers.

The distribution of the kinds of problems experienced
suggests that alcohol related family and/or marital
problems are most prevalent with 12% (or almost 9
million persons) of the respondents reporting them.
The prevalence of legal problems is somewhat lower with
6% (or almost 5 million persons) reporting them. Employment problems rank the least in frequency with only
some 3% (or more than 2 million persons) reporting them.
    Research has suggested that the normal sequence of
occurrence is for problems to appear in the family first,
the progress to encounters with the law and finally,

the drinking begins to make the individual late for work, to miss work, and finally, being intoxicated on the job and ultimately fired. This implies that difficulty in the familial sphere is perhaps the most sensitive barometer of a propensity toward serious dysfunction. The relatively low statistic for self-reported occupational problems, however, should not be misinterpreted. Powerful buffers are at work protecting and shielding the troubled employee from the realization that he may indeed have a problem. This suggests that by the time a problem on the job actually achieves recognition it has already attained very significant proportions.

Problem Drinker Profile

In addition to determining the distribution of problems through the population, the research focused on the social and demographic characteristics of these problem drinkers.

Distribution by Sex of Single and Multi-problem Persons

Sex	Regular Drinker	Single Problem	Multi-Problem
Male	61%	70%	87%
Female	39%	30%	12%

Note that males predominate in each category. The representation of males, however, becomes even stronger in the multiproblem group. Some writers have suggested that the number of women drinkers actually experiencing problems with alcohol is greater than reported. Women, these researchers believe, are even more protected in this area than men are and their behavior is most often dealt with informally, thereby insulating their problems from the public as well as self-recognition. We would

pessimistically speculate that as more women discover
the relative ease with which they can cope chemically
with alcohol, the incidence of problems will raise
drastically.

Distribution by Age of Single and Multi-problem Persons

Age Group	General Population	Regular Drinkers	Single Problem	Multi Problem
14-17	10%	7%	12%	8%
18-24	10%	19%	27%	27%
25-34	17%	18%	51%	24%
35-49	25%	26%	22%	25%
50 and above	32%	29%	15%	17%

Most distressing, is the proportion of young people who
have experienced some alcohol related problem. Note,
as well, that these problems are most prevalent during
an individual's most economically and socially productive years. Research has suggested that there is a
tendency to "mature out" of drinking problems as one
gets older. Whether this trend will continue or whether
we can expect to see a larger number of younger problem
drinkers cannot be determined at this time. The very
large proportion of young people along with the large
increase in the use of all alcoholic beverages should
signal some cause for alarm. Some of the other characteristics of this population suggest that:

> Slightly more than 10% of those
> experiencing any difficulty with
> alcohol are presently high school
> students.

> Compared to their proportion in the
> population of regular drinkers lower
> class persons tend to overrepresent
> themselves. This trend tends to be
> further accentuated in the multi-
> problem group where the proportion

> of lower class persons represented
> doubles itself, going from 11% to
> 21%.
>
> There is a similar pattern of over-
> representation among racial minori-
> ties. Minority group members tend
> to be overrepresented in each group
> with a noticeable concentration
> appearing in the multiproblem group.
>
> In the occupational groups, persons
> employed in the trades, both skilled
> and unskilled, are overrepresented...
> this pattern is most prevalent in the
> multi-problem group where almost half
> of those reporting problems are to be
> found in these occupations.

The findings of our research are essentially in
agreement with other work in the field. The alcohol
abuser and/or problem drinker is not the grizzled, old
skid row derelict, but is a man in the most economically
and socially productive years of his life. He is still
employed or going to school and probably still has the
support of his wife (or husband) and others important
to him. It is likely that the alcohol abuser would deny
that he may have or be developing a problem. A conspiracy
of silence surrounds him precluding the possibility of
any sort of meaningful confrontation. When confrontation
finally does come, often the damage to one's social
standing is so severe that only a relatively limited
range of alternatives remain. Not only does the individual have to deal with his drug problem, but must con-
sider building a new life. The implications of these
findings are clear -- people are in trouble, yet the
existent social norms are "working against them" by
assuring that they will not have to deal with their
problem until it has achieved major proportions.

XIV

Analysis
of
Attitudes

Alcohol Use, and Problem Drinking

Up to now we have detailed what people do, now we would like to shift our focus somewhat and examine what people think about what they might be doing and some others around them. In order to do this we presented all our respondents with a series of "loaded" questions concerning alcohol and asked them whether they agreed, disagreed, or had no opinion about the statement. Not only were these questions able to evaluate the attitudes people had concerning alcohol and problem drinking, but they were able to provide some indication of how much people know about alcohol and its consequences.

Attitudes about Alcohol. Our findings tend to suggest that the respondents are rather ambivalent about the use and affects of alcohol. A majority (some 68%) disagreed with the idea that..."Everyone should try alcoholic beverages at least once to find out what they are like." While a majority (56%) agreed with the statement..."If you drink an alcoholic beverage every-day you will suffer some physical damage." In the first case there is, of course, no "right" or "wrong" answer...

135

although a majority of our respondents do use alcohol, they would not condone experimentation with it. In the second case, however, we have absolutely no scientific evidence to prove that little amounts of alcohol -- even taken on a daily basis -- can be harmful; physical harm results from the abuse of the substance not its responsible use.

"A lot of people use alcohol in order to cope with stress?...more than four-fifths (84%) of our respondents agreed with this statement. This suggests that for many alcohol is a readily available, relatively inexpensive tranquilizing agent. We suspect that a large part of our drinking population does indeed use alcohol to chemically cope with the stress and problems confronting them.

Problem Drinking. More than three-fourths of our respondents viewed the abuse of alcohol and/or problem drinking in a psychomedical and not moralistic context. More than 80% of these respondents agreed that..."Heavy drinking makes people do things they know are morally wrong -- alcoholics can't help themselves." While some 77% agreed that..."Alcoholism or heavy drinking is a sign of personal problems."

A majority of respondents favored a medical solution to the problems posed by alcohol abuse. One-half saw treatment as the preferred avenue for managing the problem drinker; an additional 16% (66% in total) see a combined medical and legal solution as being most appropriate.

While our respondents were willing to view problem drinking in a humane and sophisticated context, most had little or incorrect information concerning the health ramifications of addiction to alcohol. For example, two-thirds of our respondents were unaware of

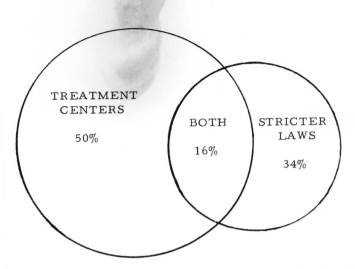

Fig. 10. Distribution of responses concerning approaches for reducing the number of alcoholics in America.

the fact that if an alcohol-addicted person stops drinking completely and suddenly, it can be dangerous to his health.* In summary, these findings suggest two directions: the majority of the population evidence a rather ambivalent view of alcohol and the consumption of alcoholic beverages; while the data do suggest that a generally sophisticated and enlightened attitude toward problem drinkers does prevail.

Summary

In the interest of understanding the most prevalent chemical coping phenomenon effecting our society, we

*If one is addicted to alcohol a drastic reduction in consumption can have serious consequences. The most moderate of these withdrawal symptoms is a tremor of the hands known as "the shakes," and the most severe is delirium tremens (D.T.'s) and convulsions. The latter can actually be so life threatening that in most cases medical supervision is indicated during detoxification efforts.

briefly discussed the history, pharmacology, and epi-
demiology of alcohol use. We attempted to direct our
interest not only at the problem drinker but at the
large part of our population who have chosen to become
regular users of this drug. From every indication the
use of beverage alcohol is increasing. What effect this
will have on our society will provide yet another chapter in the story of this fully domesticated drug.

PART IV

Summary

XV

Summary

We have attempted to describe the dimensions of the extent to which people in our society have come to rely on chemicals to assist the management of their lives. In addition, we have attempted to characterize those who regularly cope with themselves, others, and their life situation with drugs. Projecting from data obtained from more than 30,000 interviews, we believe the numbers of people who are currently or regularly coping chemically to be as follows:

Barbiturate Users	4,500,000
Non-Barbiturate Sedative Users	300,000
Minor Tranquilizer Users	5,000,000
Major Tranquilizer Users	900,000
Antidepressant Users	500,000
Amphetamine "Pep Pill" Users	750,000
Amphetamine "Diet Pill" Users	1,500,000
Over-the-Counter Sleep Inducers	4,000,000
Over-the-Counter Stimulants	3,000,000
Over-the-Counter Tranquilizers	2,500,000
Regular Drinkers	50,000,000
Heavy Drinkers	14,000,000

When we control for persons who use more than one substance on a regular basis we find the following:

There are probably 12,000,000 people who regularly use one or more of these legal drugs but who do not drink enough to be considered heavy drinkers

There are probably some 11,000,000 heavy drinkers who are not regular users of the other drugs

There are probably some 3,000,000 people who are both regular of these drugs and heavy drinkers.

In attempting to characterize those who habitually respond to boredom loneliness, frustration and stress with alcohol or psychoactive medications, our data indicate the following generalizations:

Females tend to cope with "medications" while males cope with alcohol.

Whites tend to cope with "medications" while Blacks cope with alcohol.

Persons over age 35 tend to cope with "medications" persons under age 35 cope with alcohol.

Middle and upper socioeconomic groups tend to cope with "medications" while the lower groups cope with alcohol.

Housewives, sales workers, clerks, and other white collar workers tend to cope with "medications" while skilled, semi-skilled, and unskilled workers cope with alcohol.

Among those coping with "medications," younger persons and males are more likely to use stimulants and older persons and females are more likely to use sedating and tranquilizing drugs.

Although as epidemiologists we are pleased to be able to finally discuss the dimensions of chemical

coping and to describe those most involved...as social
and behavioral scientists our findings have made us
quite concerned about their implications. Our major
concerns revolve around three separate but interrelated
sets of possible consequences...what are the long-term
physiological, psychological, and social consequences
of extensive high frequency use of psychoactive substances?

We believe all to few people, both providers and
consumers, have stepped back and asked why we are doing
what we are doing and what may be the ultimate outcome
of our actions.

Thoughts about Physiological Consequences

We do not know, nor do we have the skills to determine, what, if any, long term physiological impacts
will accrue from wide-spread, high frequency consumption
of psychoactive substances. Man is an evolving animal
and it is inconceivable for us to expect there to be no
ultimate biological consequences.

At the more immediate level, the acute and chronic
consequences to the individual are obvious. Overdoses
and physical dependences are high and increasing and
the physiological costs to both are easily documented.
For example, in our emergency room there were some
1,000 acute drug reaction cases (excluding alcohol)
during 1972. Over 60% of the reactions were from sedatives and tranquilizers.

Thoughts about Psychological Consequences

We have two major concerns around the psychological
consequences of habitual chemical coping. We believe
that the *regular* use of chemical aids to cope will pre-
vent the adoption of other nonchemical coping skills,
will retard the use of existing nonchemical coping
skills, and in a significant number of cases will lead

to the extinguishing of these skills. The problems associated with having no coping skills except chemicals are obvious. While we accept the position that at some-time anyone could have the need to reinforce his non-chemical coping skills with chemicals, we cannot accept a situation where chemical coping replaces all other skills.

We are further concerned that if one "needs" to consistently manage his life with chemicals, he will have insufficient strengths to manage the chemicals. Habituation or psychological dependency is to be ex-pected with the long-term high frequency consumption of any of these substances. We are afraid that those who are most in "need" of them are the least likely to be able to manage them and to use them appropriately.

Thoughts about Social Consequences

As with other social and behavioral scientists, we believe there are two major social consequences to the long-term high frequency use of chemicals to cope. The induction of young people into situations where chem-ical coping is the norm is our greatest concern. For example, we have every reason to believe parents who are coping with chemicals produce offspring who will similarly cope. We already have data which show a strong correlation between parents who drink heavily and their children who also drink heavily. Evidence is mounting which points to the same correlation between "medicators" and their children. Unless some intervention is designed, how many generations are left until we are all coping with all our problems chemically?

A second concern of ours revolves around the use of chemicals for social control. One's imagination doesn't have to progress too far to see a time in our society when those who do not "conform to the standards" will be subjected to management and control with chemicals. We have already begun when we can accept the somewhat indiscriminate use of chemicals to "control" hyperactive or behavior problem children in our schools. We wonder who will be next and most importantly, we wonder who will be making the decisions on who will be next.

As epidemiologists, we will continue to monitor "the problem." In the meantime we suggest social planners, chemical consumers, and chemical providers begin to determine what "the problem" really means.

Suggested
Reading

The following annotated bibliography is presented for
those who wish to obtain additional information on those
topics discussed in this volume. Most of the entries
listed are recent publications, and all are currently
still in print. Their topics include historical aspects
of drugs and alcohol use, contemporary problems in the
use of drugs and alcohol, treatment and rehabilitation,
the pharmaceutical industry, the criminal justice approach to substance use control, as well as miscel-
laneous topics on psychoactive drug-taking for coping
purposes. The authors of these works have essentially
approached their topics from a non-technical style of
prose, making them readily understandable to the general
reader.

Brecker, E., and the Editors of Consumer Reports,
    "Licit and Illicit Drugs" (Mount Vernon, New York:
    Consumers Union, 1972).
This report provides an extensive compilation of material regarding the major categories of drugs of nonmedical use. In addition to information obtained from
scientific literature on the pharmacological effects of

drugs, each drug is discussed in terms of its historical
perspective, including laws, policies, and attitudes.
The first part of the report deals in detail with narcotics, because as the authors state, their history in
the United States shows that the policies regarding
heroin have failed in attempting to control its use.
The report then continues with a commentary on other
narcotics, stimulants, depressants, inhalants, hal-
lucinogens, caffeine, nicotine, and alcohol. By pre-
senting the material from an historical perspective,
the authors demonstrate that while the pharmacological
effects of drugs have remained stable over time, laws,
policies, and attitudes towards drug use have tended
to vary. By providing such an integrated review, the
authors highlight some of the misfortunes that have
resulted from society's approach to the drug problem.

Breckon, William, "The Drug Makers" (London: Eyre
    Methuen, 1972).

"The Drug Makers" focuses on the pharmaceutical industry
and its critics. Although the author's commentary is
based on the British, his analysis is applicable to the
U.S. drug scene. He begins by tracing the historical
development of the industry and describes its organization today. He shows how a drug is made and examines
the arguments over prices and profits. Finally, the
author discusses the relationship between the drug
industry and physicians and government control of the
industry.

Carson, Gerald, "One for a Man, Two for a Horse" (New
    York: Bramhall House, 1961).
This entertaining book recalls in words and pictures
the fads, follies and foibles of self-medicating in
Grandpa's day. It describes all of the strange panaceas
for man and beast, from Pasture Weed to Kickapoo Indian

Sagwa, whose exact composition was always shrouded in secrecy -- and advertising. In sum, the volume describes the industry's big push, first from the wounds and ills of the Civil War, and later from the national expansion of the Gilded Age.

Cahalan, Don, Cisin, Ira, and Crossley, Helen, "American Drinking Practices" (New Brunswick: Publications Division Rutgers Center of Alcohol Studies, 1969).

"American Drinking Practices" provides an excellent overview and analysis of the use of beverage alcohol in the United States. The findings derive from a national survey of alcohol use conducted in the late 1960's. The approach used is essentially a demographic one concerned with questions such as what kinds of people are doing what kinds of behavior. Not only are statistics offered but the authors present the data in verbal form as well. Detailed analysis and explanation is provided for their findings. This is an essential book for anyone interested in any area related to alcohol use.

Chambers, C.D., and Heckman, R.D., "Employee Drug Abuse: A Manager's Guide for Action" (Boston: Cahners Publishing Company, Inc. 1972).

Employee Drug Abuse provides guidelines for managers who must deal with the increasingly widespread abuse of drugs in business and industry. The book offers suggestions for helping managers develop and implement drug abuse programs. There are descriptions of the drugs, their symptoms, and a profile of who uses them. Explanations of counseling and rehabilitation techniques, drug education and community programs are offered and actual examples of what some companies are doing are included. A complete section is devoted to setting up a community drug control program with the inclusion of a comprehensive list of sources of information and references.

"Dealing With Drug Abuse: Report to the Ford Foundation"
    (New York: Praeger Publishers, 1972).

This report is a summary of the findings of a broad
survey of the drug abuse problem in the United States
with reco-mendations of the activities that private
foundations could undertake. The report is presented
in three sections. Section I describes the present drug
problem in terms of heroin use in urban poverty areas,
drug experimentation by the young, quasi self-medication
by meddle-aged and older persons, and the use of drugs
as a behavior-control device. Section II provides a discussion of drug research, treatment approaches and
problems, the law enforcement approach to drug abuse,
and leadership and coordination in the drug abuse field.
Section III offers recommendations for a more promising
approach to the drug abuse problem. The staff papers
presented provided general information on : (1) drugs
and their effects; (2) drug education; (3) treatment
and rehabilitation; (4) the economics of heroin; (5)
federal expenditures for drug abuse control; (6) altered
states of consciousness; and, (7) narcotic addition and
control in Great Britain.

Di Cyan, E., and Hessman, L., "Without Prescription"
    (New York: Simon and Schuster, 1972).

This book provides a compilation of information on
nonprescription, over-the-counter drugs which can be
used in self-medication by the lay public. The authors
describe products for self-medication in nine areas:
(1) colds; (2) drugs for children; (3) stomach dis-
comforts; (4) pain; (5) ear, eye, nose, throat, and
mouth; (6) feminine hygiene; (7) insomnia and fatigue;
(8) allergy; and, (9) skin. Each section includes a
"discussion and caution" section, and a chapter is included on the general nature of health and disease. In
addition, appendices offer an array of drug synonyms
and drug side effects.

Editors of Consumer Reports, "The Medicine Show" (Mount
    Vernon, New York: Consumers Union, 1971.
Based primarily on materials previously published in
Consumer Reports, "The Medicine Show" provides a down-
to-earth discussion of over-the-counter remedies, point-
ing out those that are too expensive, the useless, and
the sometimes harmful nostrums from the surprisingly
limited number of truly useful and inexpensive ones.
The book also offers counsel on choosing both a physician
and a hospital, and some basic guides to drug buying.

Lennard, H.L., Epstein, L.J., Bernstein, H., and,
    Ransom, D.C., "Mystification and Drug Misuse" (San
    Francisco: Jossey-Bass, 1971).
The authors of "Mystification and Drug Misuse" suggest
that the increasing misuse of illegal as well as prescription and over-the-counter drugs is a direct result
of man's attempts to chemically deal with many of his
more burdensome problems and conditions. An emphasis is
placed on how the medical profession, the pharmaceutical
industry, and mass media have added to the mystification
of drugs by fostering their usage as an easy approach
to problem solving. In addition, the authors comment on
the "costs" of excessive drug use, and how the increased
use of drugs has been affected by rapid social changes.
Some recommendations are offered in terms of the mechanisms of social engineering that can alter those conditions which contribute to the misuse of drugs.

Lingeman, R.R., "Drugs from A to Z: A Dictionary"
    (New York: McGraw-Hill, 1969).
This book is a comprehensive collection of basic information, describing each drug from the points of view of
its chemistry, effects on the mind and body, medical
uses, and implications to society. The author, when
possible, provides the origins for slang terms from
both psychological and etymological perspectives. The

information is presented in dictionary format and all
entries are in alphabetical order. Four appendices are
included: (1) nonsynthetic derivatives of opium, morphine, and cocaine; (2) generic names of synthetic
opiates; (3) generic and trade names of barbiturates,
amphetamines, and combination drugs regulated by the
Drug Abuse Control Amendment of 1965 and, (5) miscel-
laneous drugs regulated by the Drug Abuse Control Amendment of 1965.

Malcolm, Andrew I., "The Pursuit of Intoxication" (New
    York: Washington Square Press, 1972).
"The Pursuit of Intoxication" offers the reader a broad
historical and scientific examination of the uses of
psychoactive drugs in the quest of altered states of
consciousness. The author traces the development of the
drugs, and provides information on specific intoxicating
substances regarding their uses in religious rituals,
sports, combat, murder, suicide, brain washing, and for
euphoric purposes.

Pittman, David J. and Snyder, Charles R., "Society,
    Culture and Drinking Patterns" (New York: John
    Wiley and Sons, Inc., 1963).
Although slightly more than a decade old, this book
brings together under a single cover, some of the most
significant social science research on alcohol use and
problem drinking. The book is interdisciplinary in
nature, drawing from studies conducted by cultural and
social anthropologists, clinical and social psycholo-
gists, and sociologists. The thirty-five chapters are
so arranged that the various parts unfold in a meaningful way. The volume begins with a discussion of alcohol
use from an anthropological perspective. Interest then
shifts to modern, complex society where the functions
and alcohol usage patterns are explored. Dysfunctional
drinking and alcoholism are considered from several

interlocking perspectives. Lastly, responses to alcoholism, alcohol use, and problem drinking are considered
from sociological, medical, and normative perspectives.

Plaut, Thomas F.A., "Alcohol Problems, A Report to the
    Nation by the Cooperative Commission on the Study
    of Alcoholism" (New York: Oxford University Press,
    1967).

This volume considers both the history of alcohol usage
and the nature and type of alcohol problems in the United
States. The book discusses some of the means of pre-
venting problem drinking, provides an overview of recent
advances in alcohol related research and the training
of personnel who will provide treatment services. A
comprehensive review of treatment services presently
available is offered. The volume is particularly valuable
in that it considers many areas in concrete, policy-
oriented terms.

Trice, Harrison M., "Alcoholism in America" (New York:
    McGraw-Hill, 1966).

"Alcoholism in America" is a concise introduction to the
sociological study of alcohol use and alcoholism. The
book is written in clear simple language and provides
a discussion of the nature of alcohol use, the onset and
development of the alcoholic illness and the effect
that this condition has upon the alcoholic person and
those coming into contact with him. Different kinds of
treatment approaches are considered. The book is particularly valuable as an introductory statement to the
field.

U.S. Department of Health, Education and Welfare,
    "Alcohol and Health: Report from the Secretary of
    Health, Education and Welfare" (New York: Charles
    Scribner's Sons, 1973).

"Alcohol and Health" is an excellent, readable introduction to the medical and scientific knowledge we have
about man's use of beverage alcohol. The book briefly

sketches the nature and history of ethanol and its
current consumption patterns. A basically nontechnical
discussion of the physiological effects of alcohol is
offered. The pathological conditions normally associated
with alcohol abuse are clearly outlined in nontechnical
language. Several divergent theoretical approaches ex-
ploring the etiology of problem drinking and/or alcoholism are offered. The book provides an excellent over-
vew of the clinical legal and administrative attempts
directed toward assisting the problem drinking and com-
batting alcohol abuse. The book provides a concise introduction to the subject matter of alcohol use and abuse.

Zinberg, N.E. and Robertson, J.A., "Drugs and the Public"
    (New York: Simon and Schuster, 1972).
The authors of this book approach their subject from
both medical and legal perspectives in terms of the con-
troversy which has arisen over the nonmedical use of
drugs. An attempt is made to unravel the mythology regarding nonmedical drug use, and why this issue is such
a major social concern. Data were collected over a six
year period in the United States and Britain from both
drug users and professionals in the drug field. Emphasis
is placed on showing the relationship between social
attitudes and a law enforcement approach to drug use,
suggesting that current laws not only fail to deal with
the drug problem, but often aggravate it and undermine
its effective regulation. Several alternatives for drug
control are provided including proposed revisions in
laws and legislation.

Subject Index